I0625395

The Audience and You

A guide to writing screenplays
with emotional impact

BY TIM SCHILDBERGER

Write LA Publishing 2024

Write LA Publishing is a division of Wombat Productions, LLC

www.write-la.com

Original Cover artwork and design by Ari Frenkel

Printed in the United States of America

Publisher's Cataloging-in-Publication data

Names: Schildberger, Timothy John, author.

Title: The audience and you : a guide to writing screenplays with emotional impact / by Tim Schildberger.

Description: Los Angeles, CA: Write LA, 2024.

Identifiers: LCCN: 2024901799 | ISBN: 9798218349790 (paperback) | 9798218364434 (ebook)
Subjects: LCSH Motion picture authorship--Handbooks, manuals, etc. | Television authorship--Handbooks, manuals, etc. | BISAC PERFORMING ARTS / Film / Screenwriting
Classification: LCC PN1996 .S34 2024 | DDC 808.2/3--dc23

ACKNOWLEDGEMENTS

Thank you to my family for putting up with me talking about this stuff constantly for years. Michelle, your kindness, and support has been profoundly meaningful. Anna and Claire, I could not be more proud of you. And Claire, your incredible help and skills with the cover creation made all the difference.

Huge thanks to my friend Ari Frenkel for his amazing, original cover art.

Thanks to Sadie for her wise and helpful insights, Rob for his detailed proof reading, Natalie for all of her ongoing help, and Tony for being a really helpful sounding board.

And a heartfelt thanks to all the writers who have shared their work with me over the years. I've learned so much from you all, and I continue to learn every day.

PRAISE FOR "THE AUDIENCE AND YOU"

"Tim's approach is unlike anything you'll find in other screen-writing books – it's *raw and honest* - it serves as a great reminder of what matters most before you type FADE IN. This book is a great companion piece for all writers at any stage in their writing journey and it will give you the motivation and confidence you need to write authentic, emotional, and engaging stories that connect with an audience." – **Sadie Dean – Editor, Script Magazine**

"The longer I do this job the more I'm convinced the most important thing you can do is forge an emotional connection between your audience and the characters as quickly as possible. Tim's book is insightful and often provocative in its mission to get writers to be more thoughtful about this crucial connection. It's filled with hard won wisdom from his own experience as a writer and reader, and supercharged with his passion for the craft." – **Mickey Fisher, Creator/Exec Producer "Extant" (CBS), "Reverie" (NBC).**

CONTENTS

1

---·---

INTRODUCTION

Welcome! If you're reading this, then you're clearly interested in being a screenwriter who gets paid to create. Congratulations and commiserations. As I'm sure you know by now, writing can feel like a calling and a curse, and the battle to get paid to write in the visual medium is ongoing and brutal. But you already know that, and yet your dream remains or you wouldn't be reading this book. So again, congratulations.

I'm not a big fan of lengthy introductions to books. I get impatient and want to move into the reason we're all here. But I do want to give you a brief rundown of what to expect with this book. Then we'll dive in, head first, but only after making sure the water is deep enough, of course. We're bold but not reckless.

Let's first be clear on what you won't see. There are no charts or graphs, and no scientific formula unlocking the secret to a great script. No templates either. No hidden fast track to creating the perfect screenplay. There already are a bunch of great books on structure, and knowledge is always useful. Personally, I don't believe in getting too immersed in the technical aspects of screenwriting. It's necessary and important, but it can also get you a bit lost, or confused, or bewildered, or worse, stuck on stuff that isn't as important as other stuff, which is arguably harder, and which this book will be exploring.

There are two aspects of screenwriting that are as important, if not more important than structure and story. Yes, you read that correctly. On the first page of a book I'm saying some things might be more important than structure and story? Am I insane? I am not.

I'm talking about your relationship with your script, and your relationship with your audience. I know, that sounds obvious, but you would be amazed at the number of scripts I have read from unsigned writers (writers yet to be represented by a literary manager or agent) who do not seem to appreciate, acknowledge or engage the audience. Likewise, too many scripts by those hoping for a career in this craft don't dig anywhere near deeply enough on an emotional level. So we're going to thoroughly explore both of those absolutely crucial aspects of screenwriting.

Before we get into all of that fun stuff – and trust me, it is fun once you fully embrace it – let me ask you an important question: *Why are you writing?*

Is it a fun hobby? Something to keep your brain busy as you work a mundane job? Gives you time and space away from your spouse or kids? Allows you to disappear into an entirely different world and spend time in the shoes and head space of entirely different people which makes you feel free, alive and like you've been on a vacation? Is it your chosen way to earn a living? Is it something else? None of these answers are wrong or right. That's not the point of the question.

The point of the question is to encourage you to think about this. If you hold any hope of being paid to write – to become a professional in this gig – it's important to have a clear, and firm understanding of why you are doing what you are doing, and what you hope to achieve. The clearer your vision, the easier it will be to manage all the steps along the way.

In other words, this question is designed to knock the fantasy into a version of reality. The more you look at this with cold, dead eyes, rather than rose-colored, unicorn-embossed glasses, the quicker you will make significant progress. The trick is to have the cold, dead eyes, but still carry the burning passion within. This book is designed to help you find that intriguing balance.

Writing is hard. Being a paid writer is even harder. Mostly because there aren't that many paid writers in the entire world. There are more professional players in the National Football League.

Talent only gets you so far. Just like in the NFL, hard work over a long period of time is required. Focus, effort, consistency, commitment and patience are essential. Dreams and passion are good too. I know it's nice to imagine yourself holding the Oscar, remembering to thank your partner, and deliberately not thanking your college film studies teacher who said you'd make a great accountant. But dreams alone won't get the job done.

Have you heard the one about the person who wrote a script while they tended bar, then sold that script for a million dollars? Or what about the other one where a person wrote a script over a weekend then sold it for a million dollars? Or the one about the person who sold their first draft for a million dollars? Yeah, total crap. Well, the first one may have actually happened around 1988. Once. And did that bartender go on to have an actual "career"? Unlikely.

But then – have you ever heard the one about the lawyer who read a book on law stuff and then argued a case before the Supreme Court? Or the one about the woman who read a book on surgery and walked into a hospital with her own scalpel and performed intricate, life-saving brain surgery? Or the dude who threw a football in the yard with his buddies, played a ton of Madden video games, watched a bunch of TV, and then walked on as the starting quarterback in the NFL? No? Haven't heard those stories? They are about as accurate as any of the screenwriting myths.

Talent only gets you so far. Michael Jordan had a ton of natural talent. But then he worked his ass off. If you hope to get to what I call the pointy end of any profession – law, medicine, accounting, screenwriting – you need a combination of talent, persistence, and a willingness to work hard. And a realistic, somewhat ego free capacity to listen to advice, learn the craft, make mistakes, grow and improve. That's the simple truth. People at the top of any profession worked hard to get there. Unless they are the boss's son. Sadly that happens, and even more sadly, it will continue to happen, and there's nothing we can do about it, so it's best to let it go, and just focus on our own skills.

I know all this because I first got paid to write when I was 22. It was for an Australian evening TV soap opera called *Neighbours*, and it launched the careers of most Aussie actors from Margot Robbie to Guy Pearce. Thirty minutes of soap opera TV, every weeknight at 7 p.m. The ultimate writing sausage factory.

The show had a story room in Sydney, where a small group of people bashed out a set of storylines for all the characters in weekly blocks. The secret of soap opera – a lot of characters, with incremental plot developments for each, so viewers can come and go and catch up really fast. There's always a lot going on, but with so many characters, no one's individual story moves much at all.

The story group would mail out the weekly breakdown (This was the late 1980s before the Internet) to five freelance writers, who would have ten days to each write one episode in the week. In other words, to flesh out the story lines, add dialogue, and a bit of a creative spin. Each freelance writer got about one script every month, and got paid $1500 for the script, which at the time was WAY more than I was earning in my job.

I was added to the roster of freelance writers, and I wrote a total of six episodes of that show, most featuring Guy Pearce. It was amazing. And exhausting.

As mentioned, I was 22. I got added to the roster six months after I cold called the show, asked if they needed writers and told them I'd never watched the show. I was given some videotapes and a writing sample to complete. They told me the writing sample was awesome, and they'd call me when they had a vacancy. In the meantime I got a job as a TV news producer/journalist. So when the call came – into the newsroom because it was before we had cell phones – I agreed to write for a TV series in my spare time. Not just any series. At that moment, *Neighbours* was huge in the United Kingdom and had a worldwide audience approaching 40 million people.

I wrote six episodes in my spare time, as my side hustle, while I helped produce live TV news. My news program was on the same network as *Neighbours*, and it followed directly after our news bulletin finished. I had the privilege of being able to help produce live TV then run from the studio control room into the newsroom in time to see my name at the bottom of the screen as the writer of an internationally popular TV series. It was genuinely unbelievable. The first episode I wrote on an electric typewriter because I didn't have enough money for a computer. Again, I was 22.

I confess, I thought writing was easy. Dialogue came naturally to me. I could mimic really well. I spent my days writing words for two news anchors and helping to produce live television and my evenings writing dialogue for a bunch of soap opera characters. Writing is a breeze!

And then I got fired from *Neighbours*. Because I got burnt out, exhausted, and my script quality fell off a cliff. I took on extra scripts because I was afraid to say no, and the combination of jobs proved too exhausting. The stupidity of youth.

I would love to tell you that early setback taught me lessons. It didn't. If anything, I never really fully comprehended what I was achieving, maybe because it came so easily. If something feels easy, it doesn't feel like something of value. You know? Maybe because I never really stopped to think about why I was writing or what I wanted from my writing. Or maybe it was because I really didn't take my writing seriously. I didn't feel like a writer. I didn't carry a journal around with me all day, scribbling notes and refining my craft. Who was I to think of myself as an actual writer? Even when I was being paid more than my day job, it still felt entirely unrealistic, or unearned, or a title I wasn't equipped to wear. For a long time, I didn't even mention the *Neighbours* gig to anyone, and I would cringe if someone asked me if I was a writer. I just didn't feel I'd done enough to earn the title.

With a combination of low self-esteem, and a fair degree of natural talent, I launched myself at the United States and made pretty much all the mistakes an unsigned writer can make, which I'll share as we move along. I've had some successes along the way, worked on some amazing projects, and I have learned a great deal. I'm telling you all this as a way of reassuring you. There is no mistake you could possibly make, that I haven't done, and learned from. And I'm still here. Still writing, still hoping, still working hard, still improving.

Since 2016, I've taken what I've learned and devoted myself to helping other writers improve their command of craft so they may fast-track/side step the cock-ups. I've helped writers find representation and watched them go on to get paid to write. I've introduced writers to producers, and movies have been made as a result, which is super exciting and gratifying. And I've established relationships with a wide range of industry folk who trust my judgment, my ability to spot talent, and my skills at helping writers improve. I'm not just bragging to make me feel good, I'm saying this as proof that everything we discuss in this book has been well and truly road tested, and has been used by writers who have improved their skills as a result, and gone on to get paid to write. In short – this stuff works.

Writing is hard. But it can also be incredibly satisfying and fulfilling on so many levels. How exciting that you have found something calling you to explore more deeply. Embrace that feeling! It's a gift. It really is.

This book will provide a bunch of simple things to consider and work on, to help as you begin your journey from unsigned writer to that somewhat forgotten extra person on the red carpet at a premiere being asked to get out of the star's photo.

Understand more about why you want to write. Make a personal commitment to work on your command of craft, not just wing it because someone said you had talent or because you've watched enough movies or TV and figure you can do this. Find patience. Avoid bashing out a draft and then get so attached to it you don't listen to feedback. But above all...pay attention to two things...the two things that are the foundation of this entire book. Your relationship with your audience, and your personal relationship with what you are writing.

The more you think about the audience, the better your script will be. It really is that simple. Well, not exactly, but that's an important foundation.

The more connected, emotionally, you are with your script, the better it will be. No, not just connected but invested. The deeper you dig emotionally, the more authentic your pages will be to your audience. The more you invest real emotions into your characters, the more they will resonate with the audience.

See what I did there? Both aspects we are exploring are intertwined. Which is why this book is focused on them. Not only are they connected, they are entirely crucial to elevating your pages from mediocre to noteworthy.

Before you ask, all the advice here applies to any and every genre. And it applies whether you're writing an independent film, a short film, a TV pilot, an animated show about alien sponges, or your own superhero franchise based on the comic book you just wrote. Anything you want to present in front of an audience will benefit from the advice and information you are about to read.

One more thing before we get into this. Now you've asked yourself what the heck you're doing with the writing caper, and hopefully given yourself a little dose of honest perspective, there's one more important aspect of all this you need to embrace.

Writing.

The best, fastest way to improve as a writer is to actually write. And then rewrite. Don't simply scribble something, and move onto scribbling something else. Rewriting makes up an enormous part of the professional writer's time. It's a specific skill, it needs to be learned because it sure as heck doesn't come naturally, and it requires practice and experience to fully command. In many ways, it's harder than first draft writing, because it forces you to dig deeper into your creation and fine tune, which can lead to increased anxiety and expectations. You can't hand a script to someone and say 'oh it's just a first draft'. People will know you've worked on this, and tried to make it better. What happens if they hate it? This an entirely reasonable fear, only reduced or controlled by more rewriting.

Anyone can write a horrible first draft, get told it's horrible, and move onto a new horrible first draft of another idea. But sticking with something, figuring out how to improve problem areas, how better to serve the audience and your own goals – that's honing your craft. Don't worry, I'll remind you about this regularly and explore it more fully in its own chapter.

And whilst reading this book is something I actively encourage, make sure you put it down and regularly scribble something. Even droning on self-indulgently in a journal or diary is writing. Writing notes about a character, or a scene, or trying a short story – whatever. The more you actually write, the less intimidating it will become, and the quicker your skills will grow. Again, I'll remind you of this point more than once as we proceed.

Okay – so now you have decided you're in this for real, let's learn about why the audience is so important, why your personal emotional perspective is so important, and how those two aspects of the craft are so deeply connected and deeply important on your journey to earning money writing.

But that's not all! We're also going to explore some other important features of screenwriting to consider as you improve your skills. I'm going to encourage you to embrace the word: manipulation, at least in the writing context. I'm going to help you understand just how much power you actually hold within your script pages, and why you would be somewhat foolish not to use that power entirely.

We're also going to take a good, hard look at your characters. You will come to understand just how vital they are, and I'll give you some suggestions to help connect them with your audience more effectively.

And I'll find a way to connect writing with sex. Because, why not?

That's it. That's the introduction.

Congratulations! You are embarking, or have already embarked, on a pursuit that will stay with you for the rest of your life – like golf but way easier on the environment. You get to explore your passions, create worlds, dive into your imagination and emotional well, and deliver stories that will have an impact you can't entirely control on people you don't know. What an amazing gift to occupy your quiet times, or your lonely times, or your need to escape times! What a gift for you as a person, and for us as a planet, who are hungry for connection and emotional experiences, and good stories well told!

One last thought. I have learned over the years that the title "writer" applies much more broadly than I realized. I have come to embrace who and what I am, and to not feel the need to cringe or be self-deprecating, even though I don't have an Oscar on my mantle or enough money to buy a villa on Lake Como in Italy. You are a writer because you feel the urge to write, not because of any perceived or specific definition of success. You are a writer simply because you write. If anyone – and I mean ANYONE –

questions that title and suggests you can't use it until you have some verifiable or financial outcome, then please do me a favor and ignore them. Be proud of what you feel you want to try and do. Be brave, be bold, be prepared to work hard to improve, and don't waste a moment wallowing in feelings of inadequacy. It's a total, and complete waste of time. Trust me. As long as you have the ability to type, or scribble, or dictate, or carve into stone tablets, you have the ability to learn, grow, improve, feel more adequate, and most importantly of all...write.

So let's get to work!

2

---.---

THE AUDIENCE AND YOU –
WHO IS MORE IMPORTANT?

I f you've ever read, googled, or Instagrammed anything at all about writing, you've come across some very well-intentioned person telling you to ignore strangers, and just "write what you know." They argue you can't truly connect to your material, unless you have a firm understanding of the subject matter, or the world, or the characters. Never mind that all of the movies being produced by studios nowadays have absolutely nothing to do with real life – but that's a separate book I'll call "What the Hell Happened to the Studios?"

This advice – "write what you know" - is not wrong. But it's also nowhere near fully right. It's overly simplistic, as most catchy four-word life coach advice things usually are.

My version of that sage advice is this: Write what you know, but make it accessible to strangers. It's the last bit that really gets forgotten by unsigned writers. I'd even go so far as to add, make it emotionally accessible to strangers. As that really is the key to engaging an audience.

As I mentioned in the intro, I spend my days working with writers, and reading scripts. I've been running screenplay competitions since 2016, and on average I read about 400 scripts every year. You can't help but notice trends and common themes among this volume of pages.

One of the big ones I see often is someone writing a screenplay or pilot based on a personal anecdote, or a moment in their past, that feels truly compelling and important to them. They are literally writing what they know, and they work hard creating something that looks and feels like a screenplay. The big problem is, the personal anecdote or moment is simply not interesting to anyone who didn't live through it. I really respect the passion, energy, time and effort that goes into these scripts. Truly.

I just wish the writer took some time to think about the audience. Us. Strangers. I want to be clear here...I'm not suggesting for a moment someone's personal journey could not make a compelling script/movie/pilot. But it has to be executed in a way that draws strangers into the journey.

Seriously – the amount of scripts I read that take place in the past, featuring a teenage kid going through a crisis – could be the death of a parent, or a move to a new place, or a struggle to come out – would astonish you. Again, these aren't horrible launching points for a story/emotional journey. But when I see them over and over again, it puts even more pressure on the execution. And when I see that starting off point – the death of a parent for example – becoming the entire script – then it's obvious the writer is exploring what they know, but they are not exploring how to make it emotionally accessible to strangers.

Anyone who commits to spending the time it takes to write a coherent script has passion for the project/story/idea. That's a super important ingredient. And if the writer is taking the opportunity to really dive into some aspect of their past that was emotionally powerful and impactful – even better.

But simply focusing the passion inward – as in wanting to explore something you know, and feel the need to get out of your system – is not enough. The challenge is to find a way to make strangers feel that passion. And for the writer to feel passionately about wanting to **share** their story, not just **explore** their story. Because that's the big, important detail often overlooked.

Here is a truth that most artists don't want to believe. People who want to get paid money to create art are entertainers. We, as writers, are really just a small step away from jugglers. And you could argue it takes more work to learn how to juggle a chainsaw and an egg than it does to write a pilot. I wouldn't agree with that argument, but you could make it.

I also want to clarify when I say 'entertain', I don't mean it has to be fun and games all the time. Some of Shakespeare's most entertaining works are tragedies. It's our job to make an audience feel something, hopefully many things. Good, bad, happy, sad, and everything in between.

If you don't harbor a dream to earn money from your writing – great. Writing is a hobby for you, and you can write whatever the damn hell you want to write. Write backwards. Miss every third word. Never use any punctuation. No one will care. You are writing to please you, and you alone. You are officially a self-pleasurer. No shame in that. Can be kinda satisfying.

But if you think being really good at self-pleasuring instantly makes you really good at pleasing strangers, and capable of satisfying them in the way you are able to satisfy yourself...then you would be wrong. I told you I'd work sex into this book, and there's a whole chapter explaining this metaphor, or analogy, later. My point is, it's important to think about the pleasure of strangers when writing with a goal of receiving cash for your efforts.

If you don't give any damn at all then the other person ends up feeling – well - like I feel when I read a lot of these personal stories as screenplays entered into competitions. A bit ignored mostly. Not a fun feeling. As if the whole experience was somewhat of a one-way street.

Being aware of other people's experiences, and figuring out how to enhance that experience takes practice. How do you deliver a positive experience to about other people without thinking about other people first?

At this point in the conversation, you may think I'm suggesting the audience should be more important than you. That you are basically a juggler, and it's your job to do whatever it takes to make the strangers laugh, or cry, or worry you may actually chainsaw your hand off. But that's not actually what I'm saying.

Before I explain, we should explore exactly what I'm talking about when I say "audience." That's not as simple as you may think either. And this is where I believe the whole "write what you know" thing comes from, and gets a bit warped.

For a long time, anyone working in the entertainment industry when talking to an aspiring writer would give advice like "read the trades, see what's selling, what's being made, and write that." I had a friend who was an executive at a studio say that exact sentence to me, in about 2003. I'm sure you've come across a version of that. People encouraging you to get plugged into the system, the biz, and to have a firm understanding of all the spec scripts (a script written by a writer for no money, but with the hope of future sale – basically what all unsigned writers do) in the marketplace, recent sales, pilots being made, pilots being sold, ideas being pitched and sold, books being sold to become movies or TV shows, short stories being sold, three words written on a cocktail napkin by a star being sold etc. By the way, I don't think anyone's called it the biz since you had to carry your mobile phone and battery with a shoulder strap, but what the hell, it's my book.

When confronted with that advice – it's easy to slip down a rabbit hole. I've done it. You look at what's selling, let's say vampire movies, and you wonder how you can re-write your little rom com set in a video store to include vampires. Or today, how you can fit your little rom-com set in a boba drinks store to include a multiverse. Or worse – you see sci-fi is selling, or someone tells you sci-fi is hot right now, so you spend months writing a sci fi story that you hate. And then the script totally sucks, because you aren't into sci-fi, and you have literally wasted time. Although writing is never a total waste, but writing with no passion, no emotional connection, is not something you want to do often. Nor is it something that will launch your career.

The advice given to me, and probably to you, isn't terrible. It means well. The person is trying to steer you away from telling your autobiographical story about that time in sixth grade when you moved house and...got sad. They want you to gain an understanding of the type of ideas the marketplace is currently excited about – in the hopes of giving you a learning and growth opportunity.

Most importantly, that advice is trying, desperately, to make you see that you are not special. Your personal story about moving house is not special. You can't sit there and think, "Yeah, I hear you, but no one has seen my story about moving house, and my Mom says I'm a genius, so maybe I'll just ignore the marketplace, and send query letters to strangers anyway."

I haven't had exactly that thought, mostly because my Mom hasn't read any of my scripts, but I definitely had a version of that. And do you want to know why? Laziness and fear. I'd written one or two screenplays, I felt like my dialogue skills were shining, and doing a bunch of reading and learning about who's buying what, or who is making what, felt like work. Not fun work. Work work. Can't I just dazzle them with my script? Why does it matter what they are buying? I thought any good script will rise to the top. Maybe I'll start a new trend of whatever my movie is about, and the market will bend to my will.

Fear – what happens if I do all the reading and gather information and discover not only are no movies about whatever I'm writing are selling, or being made, but what if it's worse. What if I get entirely intimidated by all the people actually selling stuff, or doing deals, while I sit here in my pajamas writing my sixth-grade moving to a new town script with no contacts, no opportunity to pitch it to anyone, and no real chance of getting it made? Will I lose all hope? Will I start to think this is a gigantic waste of time, and I'm a total loser for not taking that promotion at work so I could focus on my craft? Am I actually a delusional, worthless asshole?

Reading about all the people signing with managers, selling pitches, getting movies or pilots or series greenlit can be demoralizing. I've been there. The rabbit hole is vast and multi-layered. If only it were a multiverse. Not only can you get lost trying to write something you have no passion for, you can also get lost realizing the path to being a professional feels somewhat similar to climbing Mount Everest in your underpants.

In response, someone came up with "write what you know." Drown out all the external voices. Don't worry what the market wants, just take care of your own business. Write the story you want to write...no...the story you NEED to write...in whatever genre you want. If you make it awesome, or "perfect" (one writer told me an agent said only show him the script when it was "perfect," and she didn't write a word for eighteen months because she was so frozen by the comment), the cream will rise to the top. The "industry" will recognize your skills, and all will be well. Just write what you know. Control the only thing you can control. Your script.

See? That advice doesn't sound so bad when you define "the audience" as "the industry." It's actually trying to be kinda helpful. Sorta.

The problem? You shouldn't be defining your audience as "the industry" in the first place. Because you are missing the big point. "The industry" is a collection of human beings. Those human beings are strangers to you. Those human beings want to be entertained. But more importantly, they want to FEEL things. Every time they open a script, they hope it will be amazing, transformative, escapist, giving them a moment to leave their office/bed/bathroom and become immersed in something and/or someone else – just like anyone walking into a cinema with an over-priced bucket of popcorn.

Oh sure, they probably have a boss telling them they need a script they can market to this demographic, or that genre, or blah blah blah. Not much you can do about that. They'll pass on your script no matter how awesome it may be if it's not in their wheelhouse.

The more you try to chase "the industry," the more your scripts will suffer, because "the industry" can never be pinned down, is never really happy, and most importantly is never a singular unit with a singular brain or with singular desires for what they want in a script/writer.

Now we have a clearer idea of what "audience" means – I repeat, it's the human beings who read your script/go see your movie, not some random sense of "the industry" – it's important to keep an eye on entertaining them. But if entertaining them comes at the expense of your own entertainment, or pleasure, or passion, then you are "pandering," and that's a disaster. UNLESS you're being paid by a producer/studio to write a specific script for them. In that case, you write whatever the hell they want and find a way to connect with it emotionally so at least it has some authenticity to it.

You really should be passionate about what stories you want to tell. But at the same time, you need to be passionate about sharing those stories, about engaging an audience. If you simply write to please yourself, you are missing the central purpose and goal of all of the work you are doing. Once you embrace that – and don't worry, this book is loaded with tips to help you embrace this notion – you can then just go back to all the regular insecurities and worries and stresses every writer has.

Write what you know, but make it emotionally accessible to strangers. Any and all strangers.

Now that we have that all sorted, let's move onto the next important part of writing for strangers – figuring out what they want without slipping into shameless pandering.

Before I reveal any secrets, let me say there is no one in human history who has ever mastered that question 100 percent of the time. So rid yourself of the idea of perfection right now. You'll never please everyone, all the time. Or anytime actually. Can you name a work of art, a movie, a book, or any creative endeavor that has pleased every single person who ever experienced it? Of course not. Humans are complex, individual, unique, and mostly weird.

Pleasing everyone is a stupid, impossible myth. All you're shooting for is entertaining a lot of them. Look at all the stress I've just saved you. The same applies to literary managers, agents, producers, development executives, directors, actors, and anyone else you need to turn your script into a movie or TV series. If someone tells you only to submit your script when it is perfect – please ignore that mindlessly stupid and glib comment. It's worthless. *There is not, nor will there ever be, perfect, and you will never please everyone.*

The easiest way to think about your relationship with your audience is to think about you as an audience member. Apply your expectations as someone enjoying a film or TV series, and you're a long way down the track to becoming a better writer. Sounds simple, right? Guess what...it is!

Think about what you like about being in the audience. How you like to feel, how you enjoy being surprised, or frightened, or made to laugh, or made to feel anything and everything. If you feel all that stuff, you can assume strangers want at least some of that too.

As you are taking a deep dive into the story about your child-hood home moving and how you think it's a story that needs to be told – think about how you can give the audience the best possible experience.

What I'm saying here is a subtle difference between pleasing yourself and pleasing strangers. Be self-aware enough to separate yourself as a "writer" and as an "audience member." Have internal arguments. The writer in you may think a lengthy scene at the dinner table featuring 1990s Mom, Dad, older sister Felicity who's 16 and her new boyfriend Kevin, is vitally important. Your writer brain may insist the way you describe the creaminess of the mac and cheese, or the color of the wallpaper, or the conversation about Kevin's new BMX bike is entertaining storytelling...mostly because it all actually happened and you remember every detail vividly.

But what's in that scene for your "audience" brain? Is any part of what I just described, important in the larger story you are trying to tell? Does the mac and cheese represent something in the subtext, or will come back later as a pivotal plot point? What about the wallpaper? Or will Kevin get to use his bike to help rescue young you from a storm water drain in a flash flood? Because if none of that stuff has a vital role to play later, then your "writer brain" is boring the audience and being a tad self-indulgent.

It's healthy to have a constant back and forth between your creative side, and the audience side. It not only assists in keeping you away from too much self-pleasure at the expense of stranger pleasure, it also helps in reverse, and keeps you away from straight out pandering.

Entertaining an audience is important, but so is your gut, and your emotional experience. You're the one spending all this time creating something, so it should matter to you on an emotional level. We'll discuss that in more detail in the next chapter. For now – please understand I'm saying when you find yourself at a stalemate – between your audience brain and your writer brain – trust your writer brain's gut. If you think something should be in your script because you feel it's important to you – even if your audience brain is a little worried it may not be exciting, or cool, or fun, or scary or whatever enough...keep it in the early drafts. As you gain experience with your craft, and with an audience, you'll fine tune both voices. But in the initial phases, it's okay to trust your gut. "Pandering" to me means veering into cliché, avoiding risk and including mild variations of characters/settings/dialogue/actions that you've seen work in other movies, chasing the laughs or the scares or the whatevers by using things you've seen elsewhere and decided it was effective. Like using dialogue that includes someone saying "not on my watch."

Don't. Do. That. Would you enjoy seeing it? Of course not.

To summarize – and answer the initial question I asked at the start of this chapter...who is more important, the audience, or you? The answer – both. Ignore the audience and your script risks being self-indulgent drivel. Trust me, I've read more than one of those scripts. Separate yourself entirely from your pages in order to entertain, and your script will be without a soul. And that's no more fun to read than self-indulgent drivel.

I would like to say there is an easy template or graph or chart to show you how much of you and how much of the audience you need to worry about in each scene. Sadly, there isn't. It's all trial and error. Always. Did I mention the importance of rewriting? Oh I will.

But the next time you see a little video on social media, or hear a writer/actor/producer talk about the importance of shutting out all the other voices telling you what to write, and just listen to you – I hope you will understand where that is coming from and take it with a grain of salt. Yes, it's important to follow your own creative journey. Yes, it's important not to listen to some pinhead who says a production company just funded a pilot about talking sponges, so you should put sponges into your script. But it's also important to understand your job is to please strangers, to entertain. Learning that skill takes time, experience, and some trial and error. The first, important step is understanding your role, and keeping strangers in the back of your mind at all times as you write.

3

WHAT ARE WE DOING HERE?

O kay, so let's explore the process a little, now that you know
you are writing for a group, and not simply for your own
amusement.

Let's say you have an idea that's exciting you. Could be original, could be you read an article about a person in history who
you believe deserves a movie. Could be something good/awful
has happened to you, and you feel it's time to dig into it because
it's totally a limited series. Awesome! If you're going to spend
countless hours, over probably a year or two with this concept
and script, you gotta start off being super excited about it. Because if you're not sure it's worth pursuing, how the hell are you
going to authentically convince anyone else it's worth pursuing?

How do you figure out if this idea of yours can sustain
a movie/series? What do you need to think about including?
Where should your focus be?

Let me give you a little example from my currently fif-
teen-year-old daughter. I was sitting with her at lunch recently,
talking about reading scripts for my competition, and mention-

ing how many of the scripts were missing key ingredients. I also mentioned the example I used here earlier about someone writing a movie about moving house when they were young.

My daughter instantly launched into a pitch – "maybe the people move into the house, and then they discover there are aliens living there, and the aliens take them to their home planet where there are talking avocados."

"Great!" I said. And she had a small sense of satisfaction, and I saw in her head the idea that screenwriting is freaking easy – which in a way is how we should all feel when we have a new idea that excites us. Sometimes the idea seems so simple, and obvious, it feels like it would write itself. And who doesn't want to see talking avocados?

But then I asked her the questions we're going to discuss now. "Who is the movie "about"? What is the subtext, the emotional journey, the theme? What aspect of the human condition do you want to explore? How are you personally connected on an emotional level to this story, or even on a practical level? What's in this story for strangers? Why do you want to tell this story?"

Yes, I was THAT annoying Dad. But at least I asked all these questions in a lighthearted way. "I don't know, I just made this up off the top of my head just now," she said. I complimented her on the idea – and in an instant she realized that not only am I annoying but writing a screenplay isn't as easy as simply mentioning talking avocados and collecting a check.

Sadly, many of the scripts I read in my competitions reveal the writer has not thought about any of these questions. Which leads to a script that is all "story," all activities, and veers into reading like a linear series of events, namely "and then this happens, and then this happens, and then this happens." This is especially obvious in biographical scripts. A writer falls in love with an historical figure and wants to tell their story, which usually resembles a scripted documentary, with no time spent on exploring the emotional backstory. So you end up with a script devoid of layers, nuance, or character exploration/growth, just a hundred and twenty pages of stuff happening. Or in many cases, not really happening...just "stuff." This issue doesn't just infect unsigned writers. Take a moment (actually 2.5 hours) and watch Ridley Scott's *Napoleon* for an amazing example of what I just described. A massive movie, with no actual narrative thread. It's really an excellent case study in what not to do when it comes to bio scripts. We never get to learn much of anything about the lead characters, but we see a ton of stuff happening. None of the questions I mentioned above were addressed in any meaningful way.

So let us do the meaningful addressing now, because they are all just as important as your overall concept, and in many ways will drive your script's overall quality more than any talking avocado will ever be able to do.

What is the movie "about?" This is the most horrible question you will ever be asked about your script. It sucks. Because you want to answer with the story. It's about talking avocados! But that's not the question being asked. The "about" refers to all the other, messy, under the surface stuff that demands thought. It requires you to be able to verbalize your emotional connection with your story.

I spent many years in a weekly writing group – where every Tuesday we would gather in a small Los Angeles Theatre. Twelve writers paid to be there – and a bunch of actors would show up. The writers never knew which actors would attend. Three writers each Tuesday were given 30 minutes of stage time, to present whatever they wanted. They would cast from the pool of actors who were there that week. Could be the first act of a new screenplay, or pilot, or the second thirty, or third, or a short, whatever. When it was finished, the moderator would get on stage with the writer, and give feedback. Then the other writers in the room would also deliver feedback.

It was an enormously helpful experience, and I encourage you to find something similar or to create one. Hearing your words out loud, hearing the immediate feedback, from the audience, moderator and peers, was so instructive, both in a writing sense, and a dealing with feedback sense. And a giving feedback sense – let's not discount that skill when it comes to improving your command of craft.

I'm talking about this because there were MANY nights when I presented something new, and I got the audience laughing loudly. I tend to write comedy-dramas – so getting those laughs was very satisfying. Pleasing an audience is the best. So with the buzz of laughs resonating in the theatre, I would walk on stage, congratulated by the actors exiting to their seats, and I'd sit down, get my notebook out, and wait for the praise from our intimidating and often grumpy moderator. "Surely I was on the right track," I would think. "Clearly, I might be a genius. This writing thing is freaking easy."

And then…"So what is this "about?'"

I would explain the plot of the script, assuming he wanted to know what happened in the pages not presented.

He would always interrupt. "No. I asked what is this ABOUT?"

At that point all my self-congratulatory posturing would vanish. I would then babble. In the early days anyway. I'd mumble something about how it's about people falling in love, or being too stupid to fall in love, or about death, or something or other. The truth was, I wasn't able to answer the question he was asking, and all the jokes in the world couldn't save me.

What I came to discover – without a very clear answer to that question, my script would only ever be considered "cute." I tell you this now, to save you much pain and frustration. If anyone in the entertainment industry ever calls your work "cute," it is NOT a compliment. It is code. It means they appreciate your skills and command of craft. They can see you've got some chops. But they didn't connect on an emotional level with your pages, which means there is nothing they can do with the script or with you as a writer. I am not exaggerating. Cute = Death.

Do not fall victim to that perceived positive feedback. It's not positive. Well, it's not awful, but it's not nearly enough to move your dreams forward at all. "Cute" usually means you haven't figured out what your movie is "about."

What does "about" mean anyway? It's not the plot. Any idiot who reads your script can figure that out. Well, most idiots.

"About" in this context means *subtext*, the underlying emotional themes you are exploring.

A brief aside – if you ever come across a famous writer/director spouting off about how they don't think about all that heavy and boring stuff like "subtext" until they are shooting, or they figure it out as they go – please don't listen. It's total bullshit, said to make themselves seem casually genius-like. Bullshit. Subtext, theme, whatever you want to call it, is crucial, and something you NEED to have figured out, at least in a general sense – before you finish your outline because it will instruct everything in your script. Literally everything. It must. Otherwise your script risks being aimless, easily distracted, and worse...cute. I've seen it, more often than you want to believe. Scripts wandering around, filled with stuff that appears interesting, but with no subtext, or sense of what it's doing under the surface.

This applies to every genre. Want an example? The original *Guardians of the Galaxy*. Sure, it was a film about a human dude in alien lands, a large headed world, a talking racoon, a power stone and all that fun stuff. But what it's really "about" – is the power of family. The script is really following all these lonely, misfit characters finding each other, and bonding. The stone and the bad guys and all that other stuff are just opportunities to bond the characters with each other, and with us.

If the writers of that script were on stage with my old moderator – they would've answered the "about" question with something like "the power of family."

I'm not saying your "about" needs to answer a significant life question. One could argue there aren't any genuine, or definitive answers about what it is to be a human living on earth. No, the "about" answer is your attempt to show someone that you have decided to use your story to explore some aspect of the human condition. You're having a go. You are contributing to the cultural conversation. I repeat, you are not answering, you are contributing. That's a big difference I'll get to in a moment.

Whatever idea you have – it's really important to quickly move to the "about" question. So when you read a biography of some kick ass person in history, and you think "Wow, that would make an amazing movie," quickly ask yourself, "Okay, so what aspect of the human condition can I explore with this?'

I did that. I fell in love with an historical figure – Charles Kingsford Smith – first man to fly across the Pacific Ocean. He and his crew did what no one thought was possible in 1928. His aerial adventures are incredible. He had a ticker-tape parade in New York City. He was a proud Australian, which made me love him even more. Natural movie fodder, I thought. I wrote drafts. I thought they were exciting. No one cared because I hadn't figured out what his adventures said about being human. And even when I did – the idea that this man was a complete genius in the sky and an almost total failure on the ground – I could never quite mold that into something that truly connected this guy with strangers. I kept letting facts get in the way. I kept thinking I needed to be accurate and linear so strangers would be amazed about what this man could do with a plane. Seriously – you would not believe what he managed to accomplish. No one cared, at least not enough to get passionate about supporting this expensive biopic featuring an Australian, and sadly I was not Ridley Scott.

It taught me a valuable lesson. Without a firm and clear idea of what aspect of the human condition I wanted to explore, my stories failed.

As soon as you think "this would make a great script," ask yourself "so what could it be "about?"

⚜

Before moving on to the next fun bit of this pregame planning and thinking, let's circle back to answering a question about the human condition.

As I mentioned, there really aren't any answers. I don't think any great painting over thousands of years has ever really answered a question about being human. Neither has any poem, play, novel, movie or cave painting. You really want to avoid thinking you have answers to some of life's big questions. Writers who slip into that headspace often write scripts that feel like they are supposed to be performed while standing on a soap box. No one likes a lecture, apart from when you are actually attending a lecture. Even then...maybe.

If you think you have answers, then you are telling the audience stuff. You risk pointing the finger. "Look idiots, I have figured it out for you. You're welcome."

Remember what I said in the last chapter about your personal audience brain? Do you enjoy films where the writer is telling you how it is? No, you don't. (I know, I just told you what you think – I appreciate the irony). But no one responds to a know-it-all who has decided they are smarter than the audience.

When I say think about what aspect of the human condition you want to explore – please put the emphasis on "explore." That's all you're hoping to achieve. Throwing in some creative thoughts. Giving your two cents on whatever it is you have chosen to throw those coins at.

It should be more of a "hey, I reckon this is interesting" instead of "this is how it is."

The goal of any work of art is to stimulate conversation. Or thought. Or an emotional reaction on some level. To engage. Screenwriting is still art. You want your audience to feel provoked. Or at least to feel. You get to try controlling what you want them to feel, and that is a whole other chapter. But part of that is letting them ponder the observations you are making about the human condition. And then filtering those observations through their own emotional lens, based on their own, unique life experience. They can only do that if you first figure out what those observations actually are, and then give them space to contemplate, rather than just feel force fed your conclusions.

I bet when you thought how cool it would be to write screenplays, you didn't think you'd be digging into this stuff, but trust me, it's this stuff that separates scripts from the very large, soulless, and dull pack.

Ponder that important question, for now comes the fun part – figuring out why you think this idea would make a great script. That means thinking about why you – yes you, just you – are currently engaged by this idea. What part of your emotional core is it speaking to? I guarantee it's speaking to something inside you, possibly subconsciously, which makes it harder to figure out, granted, but still, the exercise is important.

If you can figure that out – what part of your emotional core this story is triggering - then you are well on the way to figuring out what aspect of the human condition you want to explore. Because...guess what...you're already exploring it. That is why you are attracted to this idea, or this story, at this particular moment.

I once had a conversation with a writer about his biographical drama. He was very intrigued by a female historical figure who did amazing things. He wrote a script outlining all those amazing things. When we chatted, I asked him what intrigued him about this person. He gave me a long answer about all the cool stuff she'd done. But then I kept asking more questions, trying to figure out what it was about her that was so appealing. Eventually, he worked his way around to realizing he was mildly jealous of her. She took risks. She followed her dreams, her heart, even if it meant being seen as unconventional, or weird. Even if it meant personal sacrifice on some levels, because she would never "fit in." He identified with those choices, those risks, the road less traveled. Sure, her exploits were cool, but it was only when he was able to focus on his personal connection to her story that he was able to focus the story on what he really wanted it to be "about."

If you are willing to devote hours and hours over days, weeks, months, even years to a story, there really should be an emotional connection.

The connection is there. No one spends that much time on something unless there is passion lurking under the surface. And that passion is on an emotional level. This story, *your* story, is speaking to you in a way it's not speaking to anyone else. It's yours. Because you are unique. You have your own set of experiences, your own outlook, your own emotional database. No one else has the same set of tools in your emotional tool box. It's speaking to you at this time, when it may not have had the same impact five years ago, or five years from now. It's speaking to where you are in your own journey right now. That is something to be embraced and explored, not ignored, because figuring this bit out is such an important part of any storytelling, in any medium.

You don't have to have everything perfectly figured out. Good grief, I wish that were easy and possible. The process of writing will reveal more than you know. I wrote a dozen drafts of a script, then turned it into a play, and it was only during rehearsals that I fully understood how much of the subtext to the entire thing was about grief. Yes, it took me that long to figure it out. But I subconsciously inserted it all the way through the process. I don't expect you to know all the answers. Just have an idea of what you want to explore.

You know, stuff like "the restorative power of love," or "the destructive power of love" or "what choices people are capable of making when put in an extreme position." You get the idea.

Give yourself a start. Something to explore that speaks to you. I promise it's already there. You just need to find it.

This is not hippie drivel. This is the foundation of every successful movie, or book, or painting ever. Name anything, and then think for 30 seconds about the underlying subtext. You'll find it. Like *Guardians of the Galaxy.* Or *Titanic* – the power of love to overcome everything (except cold water). Or *Mad Men* – where the series explores the theme of identity and it's power. Or *Shakespeare in Love* – which teaches Will the difference between infatuation/lust and love, and what that can unlock inside a person. Or the TV series *Bones* – which, despite being a procedural crime drama – was actually about what happens when you open yourself up to love. Have a look at the arcs of all the central characters over the seasons. Or *Barbie* – which I would argue is saying the patriarchy is damaging to everyone, regardless of gender, and about the power of finding your own sense of purpose. I could go on, but this isn't supposed to be a long book. My point – every good movie or TV series has a subtext, or a theme, that the writers and producers figured out before they shot a frame. Movies that fail, or leave you feeling a bit empty haven't explored that aspect seriously. The more you deep dive, the more you will discover. Or at least you'll figure out what the creator was trying to do...even if they didn't fully succeed.

Figuring out this stuff makes the next steps in the process much easier. Because all of a sudden, your script has a spine, a foundation, a purpose. Everything that follows feeds off this. Or at least it should. You quickly remove the desire for meaningless scenes where characters eat lunch and talk about the weather.

Every scene now has an opportunity to help the audience connect with characters, or progress the story. Based on your subtext. And it helps you keep a clearer head. Sometimes writing feels like standing at the entrance to a maze, with a million different choices. Having a sense of what you want your script to be "about," reduces that number by a lot. Sadly it doesn't reduce it to just one – but I did say writing is hard.

The more connected you are on an emotional level with your idea, the greater the understanding you have about your own feelings, desires and passions, the stronger and more authentic your script will be to strangers. Without even trying too much. The challenge is more about channeling all those passions and desires and energy into something that appeals to strangers. Which sounds easy, but needs a bit of exploration.

———

Before we dive into that exploration, I suggest a quick writing assignment. Take a moment, and sit with a pad and pen, or notebook, or laptop, and explore a theme that appeals to you. Not a specific story but a theme. Something you feel strongly about. Maybe it's connected to your current project, or maybe your current project is actually connected to it in a way you haven't realized. What do you feel strongly about? Love, death, the quest for "happy," the future of the planet, the way we treat pets and how it relates to our own issues, money, brown paper bags, anything.

If you have a current script, or an idea for a script, then after a few minutes of exploring themes that currently appeal, see if the idea you have in any way connects with the ideas you scribbled. And if it doesn't try to see what themes could exist in the idea. This is all about finding what's resonating with you right now. What's really going on in that head and heart of yours. Don't spend hours on it – and don't get stressed if you can't figure it out immediately.

Sometimes it's hard to see. Okay, often it's hard to see. But that doesn't mean you shouldn't try – because as I may have mentioned – it's REALLY important as you assemble your script.

4

WHY SHOULD A STRANGER CARE?

Pleasing strangers is an inexact science. Let's be clear headed about this. If someone knew how to please strangers every single time they wrote something, then they would be a billionaire, and one of the big riddles of the human experience would be solved.

I hope that particular riddle is never solved. Human beings are unique and different and special and we all have our own journeys and character and behavior and reactions to things. Imagine if that weren't the case? If we all, to a person, found everything equally funny, scary, sad and emotionally impactful? How incredibly dull that would be? Maybe helpful in some ways when it comes to writing entertainment, but still...dull.

I don't think there is any artist in human history who got it right every time. Not Leonardi DaVinci, Van Gogh, or James Cameron. James Cameron is closest, from a being-very-rich-whilst-still-alive perspective, but then he succeeds by using a very reliable model – don't take any story risks, make it emotional, and make sure the imagery is awesome.

I say this to try and ease some of your internal pressure to deliver a masterpiece with your first script. There is no "perfect," and you'll never please all the people, all of the time. Hollywood Studios can't do it, no matter how much money, time and focus groups they throw at us. Have a look at Marvel Studios if you need evidence.

By the way, as an aside, may I say I'm not sure this era of "Rotten Tomatoes" is the healthiest thing. Do we want our definition of successful entertainment to be something that pleases every single critic? Does that risk us supporting stuff than could become kinda bland?

I was a movie critic for years in Australia, for a local TV station. I quickly discovered people within the station had wildly different feelings about movies. And if you think about it, film critics come from all sorts of backgrounds and walks of life. Expecting/hoping they have the same opinion about a project is kinda weird. I hope there remains space for the 50% films – the ones that polarize critics, speak to some people intensely, and offend others just as intensely. Art was never intended to give everyone the identical reaction. It's why we have "cult" movies and TV shows, right? Those films and TV series that never find mass commercial success, but live on and on thanks to the devotion of a core group, who feel it in ways the rest of us never fully understand. Those stories matter too, and should always matter.

I'm not suggesting for a second you should strive to offend people. Unless you want to I guess. The whole point of this chapter is to explore ways to connect your audience to your material. Or at the very least, to generate an emotional reaction. All I'm saying is we, as writers, shouldn't strive for bland, or inoffensive, because the harder we try to please everyone, the greater the chance we truly please no one.

I know it sounds like I'm delivering a mixed message here. On the one hand, I'm demanding you pay attention to the audience, and on the other I'm saying it's okay to not aim to please everyone. So which is it, Tim? Which side are you buttering your bread? Let me explain.

Once you figure out your subtext – remember, that's the aspect of the human condition you want to explore – and then your individual emotional connection to your idea, the next step is thinking about how, or if, this idea will connect with people who've never met you. How do you do that? Like, seriously, how the hell do you figure that out? There are two things to remember quickly and early in your outline/story construction process.

Be aware of audience expectation, and be original whenever you can.

Please...I'm begging you...ignore any halfwit who suggests you write something that mimics something else. Don't write your version of *Indiana Jones* or *Juno* or something involving a comic book type hero battling aliens.

***

Audience expectations first. We'll dive much more thoroughly into your role as an audience manipulator and how that's not a bad thing, in a later chapter. But for now, it's important to understand you are the boss. This is your script. Every word right now belongs to you. And you have the power to make strangers feel stuff. That means your job, as boss, is to know as much as you can, what you want these strangers to feel in every scene. Every single scene. Think about it. Ask yourself questions like "what is this scene telling the audience" – both on a story/character level, and a subtext level. What do you want them to know? If you are asking those questions, you are becoming aware of the audience. And their expectations.

That is not the same as pandering to them. Or worrying how to please them. This is you, as boss, being clear about what you WANT the audience to experience with this scene. You being clear on your intentions, based on your confidence that you have the skills to deliver.

"Pandering" would be thinking about each scene from the perspective of worrying about what strangers might want, and trying to second guess that, and not being true to your specific vision. Hence, don't write a mimic of someone else's vision because at best, you'll be writing a watered-down version of something people have already seen. Would you, as an audience member, enjoy watching that?

Another handy audience related tip – If you're writing a genre film, be aware that your audience has seen one or two movies in your genre. Chances are they know what they are walking into, or switching onto. Try to avoid treating them as dummies who've never seen sci fi. Or drama. Or everything else. Understand your strangers will enter your script with some expectations for the genre. Desires even. Think someone walking into a horror movie doesn't have expectations?

If you are writing sci-fi, or horror, or anything...the good news is you don't have to re-invent the wheel. You don't need to spend the first ten pages explaining what every knob on the space ship control panel does (I've read those scripts). Or how moody and dark this mysterious small town is as the alcoholic cop enters to solve a crime that will somehow be related to his alcoholism. We get it. We aren't dummies. We've seen that. Often. Too often.

This sounds obvious and easy, but it's not. Every writer struggles with the fear that if they don't explain all the backstory first, the audience won't know what the hell is going on. So they add one more scene, or one more little flashback, one or two more sentences of dull dialogue filled with awkward explanation, or one more paragraph of scene description. And then another. Just so the audience feels comfortable with what's going on. Is that logical? Of course. Does it murder a script? Absolutely.

I want to be clear on this point, because I see this issue strangle many scripts from unsigned writers. I have my theory about this particular trend. And make no mistake – this is a very common trend. Too many writers fill their first ten pages – which are the most important pages of your script because this is the time the strangers reading your script are figuring out if you have command of craft - with backstory. You would be shocked at the sheer number of scripts I read that start with a character waking up in bed, turning their alarm off, then walking into the bathroom. Shocked.

I also see too many scripts with opening pages going into very specific detail about what posters are on the wall of a teenage kid's room in 1992 when those posters play no part in the following story. Or a writer going into VERY specific costume details, when the outfit is somewhat irrelevant. We can also talk about using scene description to hurl a ton of backstory at a reader – which I call "cheating." Cheating in scene description is when you type things for the reader that someone watching the movie/pilot couldn't possibly know. Mentioning where a character went to school, or telling the reader their favorite food, or their connection to other people in the script when all the audience sees is a dude asleep in bed.

All of this is a horrible waste of time, and shows a reader on PAGE ONE that you do not fully understand the relationship between the visual image and the written word. You are writing a movie, not a novel. The reader needs to understand what the movie is going to look like. And if they can't glean information about the movie – like an audience member – then the information you chuck at us in scene description is wasted. Worse than wasted. This is not the way to make a stranger care about your characters or your movie.

Look at the original *Star Wars*. We get a little, adorable scroll of a pre-amble on the screen, giving us context, and then a bunch of characters fighting each other, and we're off and away, never knowing what Princess Leia eats for breakfast or what the hell C-3PO and R2D2 do. It doesn't matter.

Or the TV series *Justified* – one of my favorite pilots. The first time we meet Raylan Givens he's wearing a cowboy hat in a polite standoff with a thug at an outdoor restaurant in Miami and then Givens shoots him dead. We are immediately engaged, curious, and on-board and we know almost nothing about Raylan's past.

Back to my theory. I believe writers front load their scripts with backstory and too much exposition because they are scared of their story. We are inherently insecure, us writer types, and the morbid fear that strangers will get bored is very real. This fear manifests in a bunch of ways, but in a lot of scripts, it shows itself by leaning on backstory.

I say this because I've done it. We've all done it. It's too easy. You worry that if you start the movie with Kevin discovering Cassie is pregnant, and she's not sure who the father is, then the audience won't understand the emotional impact on Kevin, because the audience doesn't know who Kevin is. How can we care about someone we don't know? Aren't we told constantly we need to connect with characters? (Wait until I get to the next chapter.) Surely we have to dig deep into Kevin so the story will resonate. Or we need to describe the world, so when it's at risk, the audience will understand the stakes. Or – the more intimate detail we give the audience on the nuances of the character, the more we are showing how clever we are, and how much we've thought about all this.

These are all very valid covers for what's really going on. Blind fear.

There's a little voice that sits in the back of my brain - next to the voice suggesting I am worthless, talentless, and wasting my time – that whispers "Strangers will think this is boring." So the more padding, the richer the background, the lower the risk.

Once people really "get it," then they'll be onboard whatever it is I'm going to do with Kevin. And it's low risk, because who is going to complain about learning details about Kevin and how he takes his coffee?

That terrible little voice must be ignored. Your entirely reasonable, deep-seated fear and insecurity must be confronted, and chased away. Or at least temporarily subdued. And it's not as hard as you may think. It just requires some hard questions, some self-awareness, and...forgive the repetition...spending some time as an audience member.

Look me in the eye and tell me you would be thrilled by paying money to see a movie, getting expensive popcorn, sitting in your seat, feeling that little buzz as the opening credits begin, and then watching twenty five minutes of non-stop character and world exposition. Ever been in a theatre and wanted to scream, "When will the freaking movie actually start?" as you watch Kevin riding the bus home from his boring job.

Now instead – let's say you start your movie with a closeup of Kevin, processing information. Then you have Cassie there...and your opening scene reveals not only is Cassie pregnant, she's not sure who the father is, and she'd previously broken up with Kevin, and it ruined him because he thought he was really in love with her.

You have thrown the audience into a movie. In ONE SCENE. Then you can start filling in some of the background about these two. Or the situation, wherever is absolutely necessary.

Let me be clear. Backstory is not your friend, not a useful crutch, and not a way to connect your audience with your story.

About 9.75 times out of 10, it is boring and not as useful as you think it is, especially when it is plonked in the beginning of your script at the expense of anything else. Think about the word itself. "Backstory" implies showing the audience what has already happened. Why would you start a movie or a TV pilot filling in the audience on a character's regular routine, or their past, when you could be using that time to...I don't know...maybe tell a story?

Let me say it another way. You walk down a busy street to get a coffee. Yes you, actual you, this isn't a script opening. You pass a man listening on his phone, crying. Like, really sobbing. You would immediately be engaged, on a story and an emotional level. And all you know about this guy is he managed to get dressed, and he owns a working phone. You don't need any backstory to be curious about what's going on. You simply want to know what's making him cry. Right? Because we humans, and especially we writers, are a nosy, curious bunch.

Why would your movie script opening be any different? The same nosy, curious people are watching your film/series.

Resist the curse of the backstory. Your audience doesn't care about that crap. And all you need to worry about is engaging them. Make them curious to learn more. Get them emotionally invested. Make them want to go along for the ride. As fast as you can.

And then you throw in accepted genre-based expectations, and your job is actually a lot easier than your insecure brain wants you to know.

Start connecting your audience to your idea by not subjecting them to a torrent of useless detail, and by not treating them like dummies who've never seen your genre. Be brave, accept their pre-conceived notions, use them to your advantage, and dive in.

But – this bravery and desire to avoid being derivative and boring has risks. Which leads me to the next bit – being "original."

I confess I do not like that word much. It's a bit of jargon, thrown around by producers, representatives, and development executives and it's hard to really nail down. It's also pretty weighty. I mean, if you're writing a little horror movie that is set in an abandoned warehouse, what's left to explore? Okay, so maybe don't set your horror script in an abandoned warehouse.

In fact, quick aside, please don't set anything in an abandoned warehouse. Not only am I thoroughly bored reading that setting, I also believe any law enforcement in any city would by now be permanently checking on all abandoned warehouses in their area. Because surely they've watched movies and TV over the years? I mean, come on now? If I was a cop, even a cop in a movie, by now when someone said they needed to find an organized gang headquarters or torture/interrogation location, my first thought would have to be "Have we tried the abandoned warehouses?"

And why are they always wet? Why are there always chains, and something dripping ominously in a corner? Enough!

Okay, back to my point about originality. As you think about making strangers care about your script, your first tendency is going to be conservative. You know, thoughts like "Well I know they liked that scene in that movie, so let me do a version of that." This issue applies A LOT to dialogue. I read so many scripts filled with dialogue more or less ripped from other movies. I can't tell you how many times I've read a moody TV pilot script, and one character says "Be careful digging too deep. You might not like what you find."

Delivering a modified version of something successful has sound logic to it. You're not going to make anyone upset. You won't offend, and you're showing you understand what works in a script. And anyone reading it will see that you understand the basics of the genre, which will impress them. They'll immediately see you are someone who would be a great fit in their writing room, or will deliver a great independent film. It all feels like a really low risk strategy to attract attention.

And then you tell yourself you're adding your own little "twist" to it so that everyone wins. You're showing strangers your command of craft, with your own little spin. Perfect, right?

No. Not right. None of the fantasy I just described is right. Your "twist" is smaller than you think. I promise. And guess what – you are never going to be able to deliver something that is as good as the person who did it first. Because you are you, and not that person. Your well-intentioned effort to engage and connect with your audience is actually, magically, doing the reverse. When you get "derivative" – which is the handy word to describe ripping off someone else's idea – you are signaling to your audience that you either don't have any of your own ideas, or you are too afraid, or worse, lazy, to explore them. Which means your script dies.

TV showrunners (the people who run the team who make a TV series), constantly say they are looking to add people to their staff who offer a unique perspective. A different voice in the room. Don't panic, we're exploring "voice" later. But how is writing a knockoff of something else giving that showrunner an insight into what you could potentially bring to the table?

The people you need to read your script can spot this kind of stuff within ten pages. Usually less. I can actually tell a great deal from page one, based on reading thousands of scripts over the years. Be aware of that. You are not being read by morons, even if sometimes you are being read by assistants fresh out of college. That doesn't make them morons. Everything you put on the page is communicating something to your reader. Often, it's something unintentionally bad, because you haven't thought all this stuff through.

Now, being original is great, but it comes with its own risk, which circles us back to that never-ending battle between entertaining strangers, pandering, and being so self-indulgent no one understands what the heck you're talking about or why they need to be there.

This one's a little harder to navigate. And it's a lot more trial and error. The advice here is to get out of your house. Very early in your process. As in, before you've actually written a word.

Have a coffee with a friend or several friends. Talk about your idea. Talk about where you see it going. Write the basic premise to a friend in an email – forcing you to find the right words.

Then, pay close attention to the response you get. Notice if you are being forced to talk and talk and talk before they understand what the story is actually about. Or, maybe you keep talking because it's clear you aren't entirely sure what it's actually about.

Talk to children (unless it's horror). I have twin girls. For more than three years in their childhood, I had to sit in a rocking chair in their room, and tell them a newly invented story every single night. I repeat: Every. Single. Night. Sure, some nights I ripped off movies. But they usually had requests. "Make it about aliens on a square planet" kinda requests. I would make up stories and characters and backstories. And I knew VERY quickly if I was boring them, or if they were into it.

You know one thing kids are great at curing? The previously mentioned tendency to fill your opening pages with setup. Kids couldn't give a crap about the backstory of the aliens or the colored knobs on the rocket ship. Get to the good part is what they would say if they were self aware enough to think about things that way.

I understand you may not be a fluent, charming, and impactful in-person storyteller. I'm not saying you go to coffee and pitch. Leave the vision board at home. It's more of a casual chat, where you kinda say you're kinda thinking about writing this script about blah blah blah. And read the room. Do that a few times, with a few different people, and you'll quickly get a sense if your ideas have a shot at connecting with an audience. After all, if you're not getting a clear response from someone who knows and likes you – how's it going to go with strangers?

You don't need to drill too deeply down into their response either. No one has to listen to every stupid idea your friends/family have about your story. This is not screenwriting by committee. You have the ultimate say. But if you get into an argument, or you find yourself thinking "you just don't understand" at more than one coffee...that's something you should listen too. Why aren't they understanding? What is it they aren't understanding? Is this more appealing to me than it is to anyone and everyone else? Why is that? How can I tweak it so we are both happy – me and the rest of the world?

Don't focus entirely on story either. Your conversation should include the early thoughts on your characters' emotional journeys. Mention some of the personal issues. Don't get sucked into simply talking about what happens, on a story level and ignoring the emotional journeys at play. Never forget, "story" alone does not make a compelling movie/TV series/script. Story matters, and story can paper over some other issues, but on its own it's not enough. Use your coffees to explore the human condition you want to dabble in and use your own emotional connection, the vulnerabilities you want to grapple with.

Ego is great. Self-confidence is great. But real ego, real self-confidence is the ability to listen, to learn, to adjust, and to understand you may not have all the answers to everything, right out of the blocks. You can only discover all this by getting those ideas out of your head and into the world as soon in the process as possible.

A quick word on security. I talk with new writers all the time who worry if they tell me, or anyone else what they're working on, their idea will be stolen. There seems to be a view out there that

Los Angeles/the world is full of writers and producers looking to steal ideas from unsigned writers who've never been paid to write a script. Let me dispel that concern, in three ways.

First, no one will ever be able to write your idea the way you will. Because you are you, and they are them. Telling someone you want to write a script about a talking dog who saves the President doesn't mean two identical scripts will magically appear and yours will be worse.

Secondly, I've been in Los Angeles for more than 25 years and alive for longer than that. I've seen series that look very similar to an idea I wrote. But I've never had a friend/coffee/meeting person steal my idea and win an Oscar. Yes, there are the occasional lawsuits about plagiarism. I'm not naïve enough to say this town is filled with angels. But your chances of having your idea stolen are far less likely than the bigger issue...which is my third point.

The moment you refuse to tell someone your idea is the moment you get labeled as a rookie writer afraid of their own shadow and not someone to be taken seriously – or worse, someone who doesn't actually have an idea.

If someone asks you about your idea, that's a compliment. If someone who actually has a job in the industry asks you what your script's about, that is the equivalent of a unicorn flying down the rainbow with the leprechaun's bucket of gold on its back. If you stand there, blink, and say you're not comfortable telling them for security reasons, you have entirely blown a moment and murdered the unicorn. You are, officially, in the eyes of the industry person, an amateur.

Think about it this way. A producer is always short of great scripts, and even shorter of great writers willing to write great scripts. The search is endless. The idea of them stealing your idea and finding a writer who is not only available but also willing to immediately spin the concept into guaranteed movie gold is a fairytale. It's also exhausting to a producer, much more exhausting than the possibility you may actually be able to deliver something intriguing.

If someone asks, pitch your idea. ALWAYS. And if, by some weird chance, your idea gets ripped off, find a lawyer and have another idea. You want a career, right? A career means having more than one good idea. Do not be precious about keeping your idea secret. You risk not knowing if it's connecting with anyone until you've done too much work and become too emotionally invested.

Never forget, if you want to be paid to write/create, you simply can't ignore the audience. You just can't. Wondering why a stranger should care about the story you are telling is crucial. And too often forgotten, or ignored. So don't be stubborn, or naïve, or overly cautious.

Know the difference between including your audience and pandering. Be brave. Don't settle for rehashed characters, jokes, dialogue, settings, scenes, anything. Never settle. You are an entertainer. Your job is to make others feel stuff, through the medium of your art. No one – and I mean absolutely no one – is born totally and completely gifted at that task, nor is anyone in the history of art always right. Be reassured by that. Take some creative big swings. Just be grounded enough to acknowledge if some of those swings don't land.

The way you improve your skills at entertaining an audience is...wait for it...*by trying to entertain an audience*. As early in the process as you want, do what you can to get your ideas, outlines, scripts in front of people – regular people, normal people, people you know, your potential audience.

If you take nothing else away from this chapter – take this. Being world class at self-pleasuring does not make you world class at pleasuring strangers. And you don't pick up stranger pleasuring skills by sitting at home alone. Don't worry, I'll get much more into this sex stuff later.

So now you know the importance of making strangers care...let's move onto one of the most crucial ways to do that. Characters.

5

WHO IS IN THIS?

O kay, strap in. This chapter is going to get serious. Because this is arguably the most important part of your screenwriting journey. Figuring out who the f**k is in your script and thinking about the best, and most efficient way of emotionally connecting these folks with your audience.

You may be wondering why I am saying characters are potentially more important than "story." Let's be honest, the "story" folks have dominated screenwriting instruction, information, and even perceived industry feedback since the 1980s. Let's call it "Big Story." Or the "Story Mafia." Or "Robert McKee did a freaking amazing job of marketing himself and his book and seminars, and found a way to rule the screenwriting world." Good for him.

I went to one of his weekend seminars in the mid 1990s. Two days of a surly man yelling at you, whilst showing graphs, charts, and clips from "Casablanca." I came away feeling overwhelmed, somewhat inadequate, but at least with an idea that there was a roadmap to writing a successful screenplay. I just had to join all of his mildly incomprehensible dots, and there it would be! Fame and fortune would immediately follow!

I even asked a couple of annoying follow up questions, and the guru yelled at me personally!

I'm not suggesting for a second that "story" isn't important. Of course it is. Neither am I suggesting McKee hasn't contributed greatly to this screenwriting game. He figured out a lot about story, and has had a fabulous career dominating the central creative narrative in this field.

Story is valuable because you need to give your characters something to do and your audience something to follow and get immersed with. Otherwise...why are we here?

But the idea there is a template for a successful script, whilst comforting to writers learning the craft and helpful as a general reminder during your outline phase, is – and I mean this with love – bullshit. It's bullshit that has thrived in Hollywood for a very long time. And I would argue it is now falling apart, leaving us thrashing around in the dark wondering what easy fix we can glob onto next.

Having a template makes everything feel easier. Industry executives learning their craft can use it as they try to figure out if a script is good or not. They can look at the structure, apply it to what McKee tells them is the complex path to the promised land, and make informed decisions. Passing on a script is so much easier when you can say that the protagonist and antagonist didn't do whatever they were supposed to do on page 31.5.

Having a template makes everything easier for the writer too. As long as I make sure the antagonist and protagonist do something on page 31.5, I'm ticking all the boxes, everyone will be happy, I'll write a kick ass script, and I can dream of driving a stick shift Ferrari down Wilshire Boulevard in Beverly Hills (even though I don't know how to drive a stick shift) with all the riches earned from the sale of my perfectly structured script.

If I sound like a guy from 1987, forgive me. We all know spec sales of scripts – that's when a studio or producer gives you a million dollars for the screenplay you wrote on your own versus when they commission you to write something – have nosedived since the glory days. Your chances of selling your spec script are only slightly higher than whatever professional sports, singing, or hot dog eating dreams you may have held. And if you do manage to sell a script – the deal will most likely not be for a million dollars. Not impossible...just less and less likely, especially as your first sale. When I say not a million dollars, I mean less than 10 percent of that.

My point is "Story" has ruled since we liked Mel Gibson in a mullet murdering people in cold blood while being witty. The three-act structure has been the universally accepted screenplay format for a generation. But it's tired now. The audience is tired of it. Subconsciously.

Take the whole "McGuffin" ritual. A "McGuffin" is an object or device in a script that is there purely to move the plot forward. If you're watching a spy thriller, it's the briefcase with the list of undercover operatives that simply cannot fall into enemy hands. Or the "ring" in *Lord of the Rings*, or the Infinity Stones in the Marvel movies. There has been a "McGuffin" in just about every major movie you can think of. It's a staple of the three-act structure Hollywood movie. And it's been incredibly useful and entertaining. For a generation. Or more.

The problem is, when you subject an audience to basically the same movie structure over and over and over, for a generation, we start to understand on a subconscious level what's going on. That means when a character says in the beginning of a movie "this…whatever it is…cannot fall into enemy hands…" we, the audience, know that in about seventy-five minutes from now, that thing is going to fall into enemy hands. Because it always does. For a generation. ALWAYS. Could this be one reason why Marvel movies aren't exploding at the box office anymore? Well, yes, but also Marvel have been churning out some pretty bad movies. I digress.

With an audience tiring of the same basic plot they've been served since forever, characters become even more important. At least equally as important as story, and in some specific ways, far more important.

But…original and compelling characters can't be simply and easily stuffed into a confusing but effective template. Characters can't easily be yelled to bewildered Australians over a chilly Melbourne weekend by a surly guru. Well…they can. But first you have to actually have compelling characters, and that's nowhere near as easy as it may sound to you.

Do me a favor – close your eyes. Okay, not yet, keep reading and then close your eyes. I'll tell you when. Think about your favorite movies, or scenes, or moments, or lines of dialogue. No pressure, whatever pops into your head. Maybe write them down so you don't forget. Okay, now close your eyes. I'll wait.

As you look at that little list, I'm going to guarantee what you wrote down involves characters. There's a very very slim chance you wrote about some action sequence in some movie – the way some car dropped out of a plane or some crazy stunt. It's far more likely what you just thought about was your personal connection to your favorite movie characters. TV is even more character focused, so the exercise is not needed.

Even McKee's "Casablanca" – are we all really going to say it was the story beats that made that movie iconic? Sure, great story, important beats, necessary part of storytelling. Great obstacles blah blah blah. But all those obstacles where character-driven. The entire story would've crumbled without characters we connected with, understood, felt sorry for, and wanted to be around.

I mean let's be honest – how many movies during the Golden Era of movie stars were successful because of the star power attached to the characters? Our parents and grandparents and possibly great-grandparents just wanted to watch their stars wander around on screen. Even today, movie franchises aren't created thanks to story, are they? Really? *John Wick* anyone? It's the characters that drive the desire for sequels. We want to see characters we love have new adventures/stories, even when we probably shouldn't. *Star Wars* anyone?

Every single movie moment you just thought about involved characters you care about. No matter the genre. From *Indiana Jones* to *Marcel the Shell with Shoes On* (which you definitely should watch if you haven't) to *Barbie*, and any and EVERY hit movie before and since...forever. Charlie Chaplin's *The Tramp* anyone? Characters are your way into an audience's emotional space, and it's that emotional space that connects them with your script. Every. Single. Time.

You could put this book down, and spend the next three days writing the greatest story ever written – twists, turns, drama, intrigue, whatever, and filled with the greatest stunts ever imagined.

If you have it all happen to pieces of cardboard with eyes drawn on it, your script FAILS. It really is as simple as that.

But creating compelling characters doesn't fit into a template. Just like humans don't fit into a template. Dammit. Not even McKee can save you. And yet too many novice writers have been far too obsessed with story, and not nearly obsessed enough with characters.

I have read so many scripts in my competitions that feature well-constructed stories, hit all the right beats at the right moments, yet are soulless, dull, lifeless failures because almost no time has been spent on creating interesting characters or even barely passable human beings, behaving in ways barely passable human beings behave.

I say again, and I will be repeating this – it doesn't matter how good your story is if your characters suck. Understand that from this moment on, no matter your genre, you are committed to creating well rounded, interesting people. You must. You have no choice if you want your writing to elevate to whatever the next level is. Must. It's the only way to connect with strangers. And it's much harder to do effectively than imagining a kick ass car chase, or super fun plot twist. But don't worry, I have some suggestions.

First, let's take a step back. The script you want to write – movie, TV, whatever – will involve a character's emotional journey. Who they are at the beginning, is not who they will be at the end. They will evolve. Grow. Learn. Suffer. Whatever. Unless you're writing *Seinfeld* – but this isn't the 1990s, and basing your writing career on one outlier of a TV series is...well to quote Shakespeare... "stupid."*

*Please note, I am not directly quoting Shakespeare. That was a joke.

Whenever you find yourself floating back to plot twists and car chases as you grapple with who the people in your story really are – refer back to your favorite movies/moments list. Remind yourself of the power of characters. Their ultimate ability to make an audience feel.

Who are the people in your story? Or the sentient sponges in your sci-fi? Or the talking shell in your fake documentary? Seriously, watch *Marcel* and see how quickly you feel connected to something that inherently cannot exist in the world, and yet that doesn't matter at all.

Thinking about this stuff is as important as thinking about your plot as you start your outline. Yes, you need to do an outline. Let's end that argument right now.

Have you ever seen a world-class architect walk up to a job site and just start waving her arms around figuring stuff out as she goes? No, you haven't. I don't think a leading surgeon walks into the operating theatre with a scalpel saying "So, which bit are we opening up?" Think the people building our interstate highways just thought "Let's lay some asphalt and see where we end up"?

Why would you think a world-class writer – someone who writes movies and TV that *gets made* – would make stuff up as they go? They don't. Now, some of these people may suggest in the media they are geniuses who tap into a muse who speaks to them as they shoot something. Or they'll brush off all the hard work they do so they can appear to be humble, creative superbrains. I have talked to enough people who have worked with enough writers who have written very successful projects to tell you for a fact that no one wanders into a script and figures it out as they go, no matter how casual they make the process sound on the red carpet.

So please don't believe that crap for a second. You – unsigned writer who hasn't made a movie or a TV series – need an outline. A plan. A moment to think about what it is you are doing, and why. If you feel yourself thinking, "But Tim, an outline stifles my creativity. I don't want to be locked into something so rigid..." I have two words in response – Stop it.

That's lazy talk. That's code for "I couldn't be bothered, can't I just get to the fun bits where I'm writing cool dialogue and awesome action stuff?" I know that, because I've thought that. I resisted outlines for years. And I wrote scripts that started well, and wandered off into oblivion. Or scripts filled with scenes that served no purpose. Or scripts filled with characters I hadn't really thought about.

You need an outline. An outline is your friend. And writing an outline gives you a chance to face all the awkward bits in your script you hope no one will notice. (Pro tip – We notice.)

Please note I'm not telling you what your outline needs to look like – that's entirely up to your process. Maybe you write a lot, maybe a little. Maybe you use cards, maybe you stick Post-it notes onto your favorite doll collection and move them around a chessboard while eating pineapple. You do you – just do a freaking outline. Know who you want in your script and where it is going before you write a draft.

Are we done with this? Can we please stop thinking this is some kind of debate, as if there are other options? May we move onto character creation now? Great.

As you think about your outline and your story, think about your characters. Who are they, and more importantly, what do they want? That question is important and nuanced.

I'm not saying *what do YOU think they want*. I'm saying *what do THEY think they want*. Haven't we all met or been with someone who was absolutely sure they knew what they wanted, and what problem it would solve, only to discover later it wasn't that at all? Why would your characters be any different? In fact, it's potentially more interesting if they think they want something, so they set out to get it, only to discover it wasn't the right thing. Or more specifically, it was what they thought they wanted, but it turns out it wasn't what they NEEDED. And you, the writer, knew that all along, so you set out a story that teaches your characters the lesson you want them to learn.

See what I'm doing here? I'm trying to get you to think about the people/sponges in your story as real, living creatures, with free will, and the ability to make decisions, make mistakes, learn, grow, not learn, be stubborn, make more mistakes, and possess the capacity to surprise you. Yes, you. The God of this script.

The faster you respect your characters, the quicker they become authentic, and the quicker your script elevates. And...hopefully...the quicker you move away from stereotypes and tropes.

Have you ever noticed that a lot of successful TV series are based on the lives or experiences of the creator/actor involved? In the old days, it was Dick Van Dyke and Lucille Ball starting from their own lives and expanding out. I'm not saying it works all the time, but at the very least each story comes with some genuine authenticity.

A lot of scripts I read today are populated by characters who feel like they've been torn out of another movie or TV show. They're composites of characters we've seen, which tells me the writer isn't brave enough to create original or authentic characters – they are sheltering in a perceived safe space of "things we've seen and liked before." I present as evidence the alcoholic local cop in the crime drama.

Okay – I admit – if you are writing a vehicle script for Liam Neeson or Gerard Butler that's being funded by Russian oligarch money that may need a little...cleaning...then yes, it would be in your best interests to not make Liam a bisexual poet with a genuine obsession with Cabbage Patch dolls from the 1980s and a fear of lightning. Or worse, someone without a particular set of skills, or a child he loves who can be endangered. But if you're writing that script, hopefully you've already been paid – in which case you write whatever the hell they want you to write and you cash that check. Just don't buy a Ferrari. Please. Or at least learn how to drive stick first.

But I will say everything I just mentioned are more "traits" than authentic character aspects. If you were describing a good friend or a loved one to someone, you would probably use a bunch of different adjectives to describe them with words like "kind", "caring", "funny", "gets angry really fast", "book smart", etc. When I talk about authentic characters, I'm talking about people in your script who exist as real, genuine people. As you build your people, the more you think of them the way you think about people in your own life, the more genuine they become. And the less need you have for Cabbage Patch Doll obsessions. I see too many scripts where it feels like a writer has assembled a bunch of "traits" in search of an actual person.

The more you think about your characters as people, and the more respect you give them, the greater opportunity you get to infuse them with aspects of your own emotional landscape. These are the people who can explore some of the issues you face, or feel, or struggle with, or ponder late at night. These are the people who can say what you may not yet have the courage to say. These people are your way into your script on a personal level. So you can avoid being strictly autobiographical with your story, and yet still be entirely connected to your alien sponges, or whatever, because they share your feelings about whatever you want them to be feeling. That emotional connection to your writing is EVERYTHING.

Who are the characters...the people...in your project? What do they want? And what is the best/most compelling way to connect your audience to your people? What do you want your audience to know about your people and why is it important they know it? When do you want them to know? How do you want your audience to feel about your people?

I know, those are a lot of questions. But they matter. And they demand genuine, considered thought. The more authentic you can make your characters and their desires and fundamental outlook on the world, the stronger your story will be. Please, feel free to grab bits and pieces from people you actually know. It's way easier to see a person you know in your head as you work with a character in your story, and chances are that real person will a) never know, and b) be flattered if they do find out.

I can't tell you specific answers to all those questions – you should know your people better than anyone. But I can offer some things to avoid, and tell you about an experience I had with a character in one of my scripts that surprised me.

A few years ago, I was writing a script, and there was a female character in it who was about to meet up with someone they hadn't seen in a while. In my outline, I'd plotted out how the scene would go, and what I wanted the audience to know about the relationship, and how this scene fit with the rest of the story, as I had seen it so far. I was feeling pretty good about where it was all heading, so I started writing the actual draft.

When this character walked into the room with the person she hadn't seen...her dialogue was instantly more annoyed than I had planned. Just the way the conversation evolved – right from the start, this character seemed more ticked off, and hurt over the length of time it had been. She just organically expressed anger. Which I hadn't anticipated. And it changed everything.

My point is not that my characters have free will in my head and that I may be certifiably insane. That's for another book. My point is, I had done a lot of work thinking about who this woman was, and seeing her as a living, breathing woman. So when she walked into a room, she was able to have feelings I hadn't initially planned. I let her speak, I let the conversation roam, and it opened an entirely new pathway for her character, for that scene, and ultimately for the script. Sure, it would've saved some time if I'd figured out that of course she'd be annoyed in that moment. But that's the gift of writing. Sometimes if you flesh out a character enough, they have the capacity to surprise you. And show you things you weren't expecting.

I say all this in the hope of inspiring you to embrace the characters in your story, and to feel excited to spend time getting to know them. Every minute you spend with them will make your script better. As you spend this time, I also politely encourage you to avoid cliches and tropes – which are very well-worn devices used to convey character traits. It all starts with your character's initial motivations for launching into the story you want to tell.

In all my reading, I can tell you at times it feels like the only motivations for anyone to do anything in movies/TV are the following:

- A recent death of a loved one

- Impending poverty

- End of a relationship

- Loss of a job thus sparking the fear of impending poverty

- This one's for horror – a trip to a country cabin

And...that's pretty much it. Apparently, in the world of the unsigned writer, these are the vast majority of inciting incidents, which is script talk for the event/thing/moment that starts our story. I'm overgeneralizing obviously – but you would be shocked and horrified at just how many scripts introduce their characters under these circumstances. Then they follow up these introductions with cliché scene after cliché scene. The sad funeral. The newly found alcohol addiction, the obligatory shot of a pile of unpaid bills. Which, may I say, is the worst. For the love of all that is holy, never put a shot of unpaid bills in your script. Ever. If you need the audience to know your central character has financial issues, FIND ANOTHER WAY.

These are all very tired inciting incidents. And they instantly make it harder to show a reader you have original and compelling characters. Remember – you're being read by people who read scripts for a living. They crave originality. If you're going to introduce a character to strangers by showing them grieving a loss, or losing a job – you better figure out some unique and amazing new angle. Otherwise, you are sending a subliminal message to the industry reader that you are walking a familiar path. And your reader instantly sighs, assumes they know what's coming, and feels less excited by your script than they did a minute ago. And they are on page two.

The way you introduce your characters is important. Giving the audience a sense of who they are and what they want is equally important.

This exposes another awkward issue. One aspect of character does not necessarily define them as a human being. Simply labeling someone as an alcoholic, shouldn't complete their character description. Maybe they are also kind, and funny, and really love basketball. Maybe they are lonely and really like smooth jazz and crossword puzzles and get really emotional when they see heart medication commercials.

I see a lot of characters in scripts where the writer has assigned them one particular trait or characteristic or behavior, and that's it. Much like Emily Blunt's character in *Oppenheimer* – she's drinking alcohol in EVERY SCENE. She's even talking about it in voice over. We really learn almost nothing else about her. It's frankly shameful writing.

I would strongly suggest as you think about your characters, consider them as well-rounded human beings. Complex, often contradictory, much more than one simple trait. You wouldn't want to be defined to the world based on one characteristic, would you? So why do that to your people in your story? Feels a bit shallow and rude and disrespectful...doesn't it, Christopher Nolan?

What would a character eat for breakfast? What do they think about in the shower? Would they use body wash or bar soap? Who would they vote for? Would they vote? How would they sleep, on their back, tummy, one side of the bed? What movies would they see? What's their favorite sexual position? Do they believe in God? Are they good at math? What scares them? Do they even think about any of this crap? Do they think about too much crap? Who are they as people?

Which is different from thinking about what cute quirks I can give them to make them stand out from the pack – like an interest in smooth jazz. Or alcoholism.

When I worked on *"Borat"* – I ran the field team on that movie, which means I was in charge of the group tasked with finding people for "Borat" to meet on camera (Yes, I have stories, but only this one is relevant for this book). I met a woman in West Virginia who ran an animal shelter in the middle of nowhere. I convinced her to let us shoot a scene where "Borat" was going to come and look for a dog to take on the road with him (and then eat, but she didn't know that bit). We shot the scene, but it didn't make the movie.

When things went a bit wrong, the woman got upset and the police were called – I was told by our original director to chat with her until the police arrived. He wanted to film what happened. I was standing at this woman's door, which was mostly closed, in the middle of nowhere West Virginia, trying to keep her calm and engaged.

I asked her what she liked to do for fun. Now remember, this is a woman in the wilds of West Virginia, who spends her days rescuing dogs and various other animals, giving them shelter, and helping them find safe new homes.

The first response to my question – she enjoyed deer hunting. Killing animals for relaxation.

I confess I didn't know how to respond to that. I struggled to understand how she could compartmentalize her headspace that way. I still wonder about it. Working on that movie was an amazing lesson when it comes to understanding the human condition.

Humans are remarkably complex. We often hold contradictory viewpoints in the same brain. We are not perfect. We can be kind and cruel. Loving and horrible. Honest and dishonest. We are ongoing works in progress. We are constantly aging, evolving, being shaped by our relationships, our life experiences, our desires, our wins, our losses, all of it. We are hard to define, and always shifting. But we are also capable of fundamental foundations of character. Some of us are inherently kind. Some are inherently assholes. Or manipulative con men. Or deeply religious. Some of us feel compelled to be in or near the ocean. Some of us really love math, others really love plumbing. You get the idea.

But what we are definitely not, is one, singular "trait". So why would you put a character in your movie who is simply "an alcoholic" or "broke" or "sad because their spouse left?" And build a script around that? Humans are fascinating. And the more fascinating you can make the humans in your script, the more fascinating they will be to us, your audience. The driving reason you are creating this character in the first place.

I know it may not sound as fun as plotting a spectacular stunt, or amazing story diversion. But it becomes more fun the more you practice. And it really is hugely important for your writing.

The more you settle for established character trait tropes, the more you risk your script sinking like a stone. The more time you spend letting the audience be intrigued with your people, the more they will forgive the occasional plot hole.

Taking on this aspect of writing also means exposing yourself to more people and their stories too. The more people you meet and experiences you have, the richer your story and character tool box. You can learn a lot from watching movies, but you also learn a lot by leaving your home. Go on a road trip. Show up at a convention. Deliver food or drive for Uber. Work a polling station on election day. Launch yourself into the world, and the world will deliver things you cannot possibly imagine. You are a writer, and your job is exploring the human condition. So meet more humans. Just don't be weird about it.

I want to point out here another challenge with creating original, authentic characters is finding new and innovative ways of delivering information to the audience. In the shortest time possible. We're going to discuss some of this in the next chapter, but as it applies to characters, there is an interesting side effect to more character thought. It's the desire to include all of your thinking in your script. It's the desire to front load your pages with all sorts of enlightening character moments. You know this person forward and backwards now, and you are excited to share all of it with your audience in your opening pages. You want them to understand the person as well as you do. And you will start thinking that will make the story even more compelling. As we discussed in the previous chapter – resist that urge!

It's entirely understandable. Who wouldn't want to show off all the work they've done, creating a fully rounded human being? But if you stuff your opening pages with all this knowledge, you will bore your audience. They will start to wonder why they are here. When are you going to have this complex human actually do something, or make a decision that launches something resembling a story?

The challenge is to do all the work, and then infuse your script with all that work, without us noticing. Have all that work serve your story and your character's journey. Only tell us what we absolutely need to know at any given time, in order for their journey and the story to make sense. This is an exercise in self-discipline. Just because you know stuff, doesn't mean you have to share stuff.

Yes, I acknowledge I'm suggesting you do a bunch of work that your audience may never see. It sounds really annoying, I know.

But trust me on this – your audience will see/feel all the work you've done. The more you know your characters, the more authentic all of their words, actions, and decisions will be. The audience will pick up on that. Glimpses and snapshots are all we need. They're all you need when you watch something. Embrace the challenge. How to best give the audience what they need to know about your people, in the shortest imaginable time/page count. Discipline and focus are demanded. Glimpses and snapshots. Once you surrender to this process, I promise it gets more fun. It's a game you play with your audience. It's way more interesting for us than drowning the pages in intimate details about a character's morning routine. Glimpses and snapshots. Sounds like an album title from a 1980s big hair techno band...but it works. Trust your work, trust the process, trust that your authentic knowledge of your people will naturally be infused into your pages. Because it will.

I'm not just talking about your leads. Everyone you decide you want to have utter a line in your project deserves some thought because they are opportunities. Every single one of them presents an opportunity to be memorable characters in their own right. They still hand out best Supporting Acting Oscars, remember? More interesting supporting characters also deliver opportunities for interactions that reveal new information about your central characters – how they relate to the world, how they communicate, how they give and receive information. Small details but important. The audience is always alert, seeking new information. You are when you watch something. Every single moment becomes an opportunity for you as a writer. Embrace that opportunity. It also gives you an opportunity to insert more entertainment. A great example is in the rom com *"Palm Springs"* – which I think is a great script on many levels. The bartender at the wedding only has a handful of lines, but each interaction is memorable, funny, and entertaining. The script could've had her say nothing at all, or simply react to what the main characters were asking/doing. The writer thought about that character, and used the opportunity to create someone memorable for us.

If you find yourself writing a scene with a character chucking keys to a valet, and the valet saying "yes sir," then you have to ask yourself why that speaking part exists, and is there more you can do with it. Is there something in the way the central character interacts with this service person that informs the audience on who they are, and how they operate in the world. Are they kind, disrespectful, awkward?

You don't have to spend three pages of your script on an exchange with a valet, unless it's crucial to your story or your central character. My point is every situation is an opportunity to show your audience you understand humans are complex, and behave in interesting ways. And every conversation is an opportunity. No...every conversation MUST be an opportunity.

Otherwise, what the hell is it doing in your script? Every single moment is delivering information about your people, and how they move through the world, which helps connect us and makes it easier to understand the bigger decisions your people will make as they navigate their way through your story, and their own emotional journey. The more you understand and embrace the idea that every moment counts, because the audience is always paying attention, the more focused your script will immediately become.

Who is in your story? Who are they as people? What do they think they want? What is their emotional journey? Who are they at the start, and who do you want them to be at the end? They should change during your script. They should evolve, learn a life lesson, be changed forever, maybe in big ways, maybe small. Otherwise...why are we here? If they can simply go back to being the person they were on page one, are you delivering a compelling script? Also, how are you, yes you, connected emotionally to your characters? How are they exploring feelings and emotions you can relate to personally? How emotionally vulnerable are you through the prism of these characters? The answer should be: A LOT.

Time for another quick writing exercise – as you construct your outline (remember, you really need to do an outline), take a moment, or an hour, open a different document, or a fresh page in your notebook, or a new set of Post-it notes, and think about your characters' emotional journeys. Think about who they are when we meet them, and who they will become when you have finished your script. Get it clear really early how you want them to be changed forever by whatever it is you plan on doing to them. It's a great way to get ahead of the curve early, because if you don't know this, nothing else really matters. And if you think this hippie stuff doesn't apply to your action comedy – think about how John McClane evolved in *Die Hard*. Take a break from plot, and just focus on your people and their emotional changes. While you are there, jot down some adjectives you think apply to your characters. Words like "kind" and not "pretty but she doesn't know it." Never write that. Anywhere. Ever. I'm serious. Ever. It's not only sexist, but anyone who is pretty will tell you they knew it pretty early on.

Characters are as important as story. Characters are more important than any structural template. Characters connect you with your audience. Characters connect you with your favorite films and TV series. Characters are more than a series of traits. Not all characters deal with emotional stress by becoming alcoholics. And if you show a shot of unpaid bills to reveal impending poverty/financial crisis...then to quote Shakespeare again... "come up with something else, you lazy, dull, turnip headed git."*

*Again, this is not a genuine quote from Shakespeare. For all I know, he may have loved turnips. Although why anyone would is a total mystery to me.

6

---·---

EVERY SINGLE WORD
MATTERS!!

W e're going to continue the theme of making every word count. But in new, and exciting ways.

By the way – a quick reminder that to be one of the very best writers on the planet – someone who actually gets paid to create entertainment for the masses – you need to do a lot of work, and take this whole thing really seriously. Talent gets you to a certain point, but embracing the grind is really what elevates you from the pack. I know it's not sexy, and it's not quick, or easy all the time. It's a job. Not a fantasy. And part of that job is rolling up your sleeves, and making yourself accountable for every single word in your script. Sounds obvious, I know…but it's rarely taken seriously. Instead, I regularly see it dodged, avoided, pushed aside, or underappreciated. Let's agree to end that now.

This is the part of the book where you take a good, hard look at yourself in the mirror, and make the decision to really work on improving your command of craft. No more excuses, no more gazing into the sky and imagining global adoration for the first draft of the half idea you thought about last weekend. First, let's be honest. There is no global adoration for movie or TV writers who don't direct. Can you name one top "Hollywood" screenwriter? Anyone? Currently living or even dead? Someone who only writes – and no cheating with Tarantino or Christopher Nolan, or someone like David Mamet who made his name as a playwright. Aaron Sorkin maybe – but he directs now too. Ever seen a writer who has never directed on the front cover of any magazine? Or a writer's name "above the title" on a poster, or when the opening credits role?

Novel authors get covers. Stephen King, we've heard of. Not scriptwriters. Not now, not before, maybe not ever. As this is my book, and I can make the occasional rant, I will say it bothers me how little respect we get for what we're doing here. No one would think to bring on four more writers to rewrite a novel from someone who has previously written successful novels. But that happens with studio scripts every day. It's probably happened three times since I began writing this paragraph.

Film is a director's medium. Apparently they are the gurus who wave all the magic dust around and create genius from what the world assumes was a script resembling Scrabble-letters-grabbed-out-of-a-bag-and-thrown-on-a-page-like incomprehensible jumble, quite possibly typed by an angry monkey with a learning disability. Directors are the real geniuses ladies and gentlemen. Bow to their magnificence and enjoy seeing "A film by..." above the title of many films. They possess remarkable abilities to bring words and scenes and characters to life all by themselves with no help from anyone at all. Amazing! I bet if you surveyed moviegoers right now, a giant percentage would tell you they thought all movies were written and directed by the same person. It's awful, and it's disrespectful to the craft of screenwriting and to writers.

TV is more of a writer's medium – but again, when was the last time you rushed to watch the new thing by that TV writer/showrunner you love? They may get more industry love and power, but they still aren't household names.

Even more galling to me is when an older director is given an obscene amount of money by a streamer to make their 3+ hour opus from a script they wrote – despite having no genuine or recognized talent in the writing department. We get to watch a bloated, expensive, beautiful looking pile of dog shit. And we are assured that it's genius. We're told specifically. I'm not mentioning any names. Certainly none that begin with the letter "S" and ends with corsese.

Okay, rant over. Just rid yourself of the fanciful notion you will be the one who breaks through and gets treated with the respect all writers in all other fields get a bit more of. Lose that dream now. Instead, replace it with the dream that someone will pay you thousands and thousands of dollars to buy your script, and then hand it to someone else. Or you'll earn thousands rewriting someone else's script, which neither of you will get credit for, because three other teams were previously involved, and there are only so many spaces the union makes available for writing credits.

This is a very long-winded way of saying if you are writing for the fame and attention – please pick something else. Maybe learn the guitar. Or how to paint. If you are writing to earn your fortune...please have a backup job or a career-oriented spouse/partner/parent while you toil and wait. It's time to get real – with the grind involved, the expectations, and the realities of the industry.

Which means now is the moment you realize you're not doing this for any of that. Oh sure, it would be lovely to be on a panel discussing your movie and have the audience not keep asking the director why he/she made the creative decisions you put in the script. That's a realistic dream, I guess. But otherwise, understand and appreciate you are doing this because you freaking love it. Because it's inside you. Because it won't let you go, otherwise you would've become an accountant ages ago. Writing won't quit you. The ideas keep buzzing around, the desire to scribble something or type something lurks constantly, and not writing just seems way harder and less satisfying a life than writing.

At least that's how it is for me. Damn it.

Understanding why you are doing this, and what you want out of it is a big part of what this chapter is all about. Because the next thing you should probably acknowledge/understand, is that while you are writing your spec script – again – that's a script no one is paying you to write – you are GOD. You are in total and absolute control. No one can tell you what to do. No one can push you off your vision. Hopefully someone will give you feedback and you will listen because it's probably helpful – but otherwise - understand and embrace the fact you have total control. This sucker is all yours.

Why should you embrace your divine power over this script? Because it's the first step toward owning everything in the script. And it's the first step to understanding you are not only solely and completely responsible for every single word, you are also solely and completely responsible for something arguably even bigger – the audience and their emotional state.

You, my friend, have all the power. All of it. Oh sure, some director will come along at some point and make it look like they are the reason your movie works. But here's a secret Hollywood doesn't want you to know. Are you ready? The biggest secret in this book, buried in chapter five, because that's how I roll.

It is almost impossible for a director to make a bad script into a good movie. And it is almost impossible for a director to make a bad movie out of a great script. I will fight anyone over this, although I will consider a stupid director can do a lot of damage to a great script, but still never entirely ruin it.

Read what I just wrote a second time. You want proof? I present to you Gwyneth Paltrow winning an Academy Award for Best Actress in *Shakespeare in Love*. Let's be fair – Ms. Paltrow is an entirely serviceable actress. Genuinely fine. Not awful. But no one would ever accuse her of being Meryl Streep. Yet she has an Oscar. For Best Actress. How did that happen? She got to be in a movie with a bulletproof script. And she had a director who could not have screwed it up, no matter how many times he cast Ben Affleck and told him to have a crack at an English accent some of the time.

Anyone in that role would've won the Academy Award. Literally anyone. As proven by Ms. Paltrow grabbing the trophy.

My point in all this is that you have tremendous power, even if the industry won't acknowledge it. You can whine about that, or you can focus on trying to write bulletproof scripts. And that process starts with you owning the fact you are GOD of your script. You are responsible for every single word. Not most of them. All of them.

I know what I'm saying may sound obvious. Of course you are responsible for every word, you're typing them, right? But in reality, we both know there are scenes in your script, and lines of dialogue, and scene description, that you have trouble justifying. But you know the following scene is awesome, so hopefully readers won't notice the soft spots. Spoiler alert...we always notice.

I recently directed my first play from a screenplay of mine that I modified to work better on the stage. I've never directed a play before, and I was lucky to have three incredible and very professional actors on board. From day one of rehearsal, I was peppered with questions by the three of them. It was constant, it was incredibly detail oriented, it was relentless, and it was exhausting. "Why would he say that word here?" "Do you think she would react that way?" "What's the meaning underneath this exchange?" And on and on and on. I was forced to justify, and explain every single word. There was nowhere to hide. And there certainly was no place for answers like "It's there because it sounded cute." or "I don't know, just shut up and read it."

I would've lost the actors' trust and confidence in a moment.

I'm not suggesting every answer I gave was "right." We had regular and thorough discussions, and I often compromised, and changed or cut some dialogue. But at least I was able to begin the conversation by showing them I had a clear understanding of what my intentions were with every word, every moment, every scene. That was a great relief because I've had other moments in other scripts where I have struggled to explain some of the most basic questions...because I hadn't thought my script through. I hadn't taken full ownership. I wrote it because I thought it was cute, and people would see my talent and give me the next studio blockbuster to rewrite.

When I say you are GOD and you need to own every word, I mean it. I see scripts every day where I can tell a writer hasn't thought it through. Maybe they got bored and didn't finish an outline and just kinda dived into the draft, so the story wanders all over the place, and character motivations become fluid and odd and they also wander all over the place.

Maybe the writer just didn't want to dig deeply enough emotionally...so they kinda talk around issues or swerve away from genuine human emotion by throwing in a fart joke. I've done that.

Or maybe they were just a bit lazy. Or didn't want full ownership, just figured they'll be re-written anyway, so why bother? Whatever the reason, the script is nowhere near as impactful as it could be, and the reader feels a little like their time has been wasted. If the writer isn't going to take this seriously, why should the reader?

The good news is none of this is as intimidating or terrifying or grindingly dull as it sounds. Well, it can get a little dull – but mostly from the perspective of "Ugh, do I have to answer every question in this script – can't AI just insert some stuff while I watch *Black Mirror*?"

Once you embrace your absolute and total power over your script and your audience, it can actually be quite liberating. Now that you feel that power and control and sense of total creative freedom...here is the first thing you should do.

Write an outline. Yep – I'm back nagging you about the outline. And you thought I was done with all that.

My process...I write longhand in notebooks at coffee shops. I have conversations with myself about what I'm doing, what I want to say, and how best to say it. I find the slower pace of writing each word by hand, versus typing too quickly, gives my brain a chance to contemplate what I'm saying. This makes my outline slightly less likely to veer off into some sort of terrible story or character hole. But that's just me, and I often find myself focusing more on what goes on in a scene, so I have to step back and remind myself who is in my story, what do they think they want, and what are they willing to do to achieve their perceived goal (that will ultimately not really be what they want/need).

Here is where an outline really shines. You get a moment to really think about every single aspect of your proposed script. Even snippets of dialogue if that helps. The outline is the place where you explore all the stupid ideas. It is the place you allow yourself little tangents, the little moments where you decide for an hour to look at everything from the perspective of an entirely different character. Or where you wonder if the tone should be less *Pulp Fiction* and more *John Wick*. Or maybe the idea should be a musical? And you get to have all these fanciful, and mostly entirely dumb thoughts without letting them get anywhere near an actual script. Outlines save you soooo much time. I have another secret about writing to share – but first – let me give you one more benefit of writing an outline as you embrace being GOD of your script.

The audience. What the f**k do you want them to feel? We're about to get into that in much more detail in the next chapter – but let me say in advance that the outline phase is the time you figure out what every scene is delivering to your group of strangers. Trust me – you don't want to be figuring that out after you have a draft. The outline is the time. But I'll dive into that shortly. First, a secret you may not be aware of.

I don't know how many scripts you've written. Whether it is "almost one" to "twenty seven" – there is one common feeling every writer has when the first draft is finished. Now let me point out I said *feeling*, I didn't say *fact*. It's safe to say every writer quietly and secretly hopes the draft they wrote is perfect and will be recognized as such, and therefore, no rewriting will be required.

Oh sure, some writers will say they love rewriting – and I can definitely say I have grown to appreciate its power and purpose over the years. It can really take the pressure off a first draft. I'll discuss rewriting in way more detail later.

Typing "the end" on any draft at any time is always an achievement, something to be celebrated. You stuck at a task, worked hard, and actually generated a bunch of pages that pretty much have a beginning, middle and end, and tell a story. Hooray!

I imagine when I finish the first draft of this book, I will bask in a warm glow of stick-to-itiveness and be impressed at my achievement. It's human, it's natural, it really should happen, and it can totally and utterly screw up your script.

If you are relatively new to screenwriting, and you decide to forgo the outline phase because it's boring, and hard, and you write much more creatively when you're in the zone, and actually in the script and the dialogue is guiding you – then your first draft carries a lot of extra weight. Let me say again, any successful writer who tells you that's the way they write – is lying. They may not call their prep work an "outline" – but they do a ton of prep work. Or...they generate truly terrible first drafts, but are comfortable and committed and skilled at the rewrite process.

New writers are not comfortable, committed or skilled at the rewrite process. How could you be? Which means you have an outline free first draft that is guaranteed to be truly awful. Guaranteed. As in, no doubt at all. And not only do you have a hot garbage draft, you also have a very inflated, yet oddly justified sense of achievement. Which means you have a great deal of affection for the hot garbage draft, and you aren't yet aware just how terrible it is.

Which makes you reluctant and somewhat resistant to blowing it up and starting again. Somewhat hesitant to fully comprehend just how hot garbage-esque it is. That's human nature. Why wouldn't you love your first creation? We all love our first born child more than the subsequent children, don't we? I'm kidding... but as it applies to scripts...I'm deadly serious.

The quicker you learn this secret – that no matter how much you tell yourself you're going to be a re-write beast so you can skip an outline and barrel straight into the garbage draft – you will fail. Because it's human nature.

You will assure yourself you'll change everything, and that's totally fine. But when you type "the end" on your baby – all that rational thought flies out the window, vanishes in the time it takes you to open your celebratory beverage, or yell to your wife or call your Mom or whatever you do to acknowledge your crowning achievement. "It's not THAT bad," you'll tell yourself. "There's a lot in here that really hangs together. Maybe just a few tweaks."

And thus begins the inevitable delay in your writing journey. In a moment, you are thinking more about personal pride than audience entertainment. You're thinking more about hope and optimism and less about hard work and practice. The sense of satisfaction and pride in actually finishing something that takes a lot of time and energy overwhelms everything.

So don't tempt yourself until you feel confident, and ready, and fully and completely armed with a road map...otherwise known as an OUTLINE. Why tempt the Completion Devil? Why mess with all those feelings of love and affection for your disfigured, barely recognizable pile of hot garbage you are telling yourself could quite possibly be genius?

It is all a colossal waste of time. Because your second draft will not be different enough. You'll hang onto crap you should've shed in the outline phase, but now it's a fully realized scene, you think it's worth keeping. You won't hear the feedback in the same way. You won't listen. Because you love your little baby. Your creation. And again...you are WASTING TIME.

Even with an outline, your first draft will probably suck. They usually always do. But going through the process of writing an outline in some way detaches you from the draft. Because writing the actual draft is more like following a map – not launching into the wilderness with a machete and seeing if you can find the magic waterfall. You always know where you are, which is more boring but effective. You always know where you are going because the hard work was done building the map. As a result, the draft doesn't feel like quite the same level of incredible achievement. It's still awesome, and rewriting still sucks – but you've already committed to the process, so it just feels easier to start from scratch.

Embrace your absolute power. Explore all your options during the outline phase. So that when you write a draft – every word counts. Every word. Not every second word. By the time you finish your draft, you can justify, explain, defend, argue for, or concede defeat on everything that happens. When someone asks why your sentient sponge likes eating popcorn, you not only know exactly why, but you can talk about how the popcorn represents the love and affection the sponge didn't receive on its home planet and it is now consuming it in an exaggerated way to try and fill that emotional hole (subtext). That may be stupid – but it's your stupid, and it's there because you thought it all through. If it turns out to actually be stupid, then you can adjust, because you know what you want to say.

Understanding your power and total control over your script also helps with brevity. Brevity is GOD. Maybe a co-God with you. As you embrace the idea that every word matters, then every word earns its place. Every word needs to present itself to you for your approval. Every "and" or "yes" in dialogue. Every "she puts the sword" or "the field is as brown as a canvas sack made by a Middle Eastern woman with hearing problems" in your scene description. Every "Cut To" (which doesn't need to be there in the first place). Every single word earns its place in your precious script. You own the most valuable computer page real estate ever. No wasted words. Not. One. Which means ditch the deaf Middle Eastern woman and write "the brown field."

One quick tip that seems appropriate when discussing brevity: The overuse of words ending in "ing" in scene description. Try to avoid where possible. If you have a character eating, or sitting, or walking, try to have them sit, eat, walk. Not only does it make the action feel more present and active, it also makes every sentence cleaner, shorter, and easier to read. Try it – you'll be amazed how often you use "ing" words, and how removing them makes everything feel better.

Every word counts. And don't be afraid to use a thesaurus. They exist to help writers sound less boring and more...astute. (I looked up words for "smart"). Once you fully embrace that, along with your power, you are ready to embrace the next exciting secret – "manipulation" is not a dirty word in writing.

7

— . —

WHY "MANIPULATION" CAN BE A GOOD WORD

The word "manipulation" gets a bad rap sometimes. Oh sure, when it's used to describe an intimate relationship, it sucks. But when it's used to describe physical therapy, it's pretty good, right?

When it comes to screenwriting, I'm going to bet there are a bunch of artists who will tell you the very idea of manipulating your audience is disgraceful. Or mean-spirited. Or wrong. As if you are somehow being awful to your people. Purposely exploiting their desire for entertainment, and bending their emotional states to your will. How terrible.

No. How perfect.

If you just tuned into this book and somehow missed everything that's gone before – then welcome. Maybe skip back a bit when you're done with this chapter. But if that's the case, you have missed my various mentions that we, as writers who want to get paid to write, are entertainers. We are not far removed from jugglers, or magicians, or even the guy standing on a street corner waving a sign with a word or two on it, hoping someone will read it, and act upon the information received. Entertainers. It's well past time we acknowledged and accepted that fact.

If you want to earn money writing, you have to initially entertain your readers and ultimately your audience. If you are unable to accomplish that feat, you will not receive money to write. You will be a hobbyist. There is no shame in that – it can be an enjoyable pastime and I wish you all the best with it. But if you want money, you gotta entertain.

A HUGE part of entertaining your audience, is taking hold of their emotional state, and manipulating it. Bending it to your will. Making strangers feel what you want them to feel, when you want them to feel it.

This applies to all genres. I'm not for a moment implying the word "entertaining" should only mean pleasant, happy feelings. Horror? Obviously – if you can't make strangers scared as they watch a woman walk through a dark house carrying a candle – then what are you doing? If you can make strangers feel a sense of foreboding and fear, simply by watching a woman they will never meet, who doesn't even exist in real life, walk through a dark house holding a candle, then you have achieved total emotional manipulation. Kudos to you.

This chapter is all about getting you to embrace the concept of manipulating your audience. Not only getting to the point where you are okay with the idea, but actually excited, and up for the challenge. Remember, you are GOD of your script. You get to decide what happens, and what people know and feel at any given moment. A huge part of that power lies in your ability to make the audience feel things. Genuine feelings. Not simply the "Ha ha, I see what you tried to do there" kinda acknowledgement. Genuine, human emotions.

So let's embrace the word, and work on your manipulation skills. I should stress for legal purposes, everything I will discuss here is designed purely to be used in works of creative fiction. Not in real life. Please don't use the powers you are about to be given for evil in your actual life. That would be stupid and unnecessary. Save it for the page! Also, for the record, I was making a joke about the whole "for legal purposes" thing, in case you worried.

There are ways to mess with your audience's emotional state both large and small. And it's useful to always be thinking on both levels. Which means don't write a bunch of dull scenes, then throw in some huge emotional moment, and expect that to make up for the desert your audience just wandered through. Large and small. Every single scene. Always be aware of what you want your audience to be feeling, and how you can tweak those feelings. Or contradict them. Or alter them in unexpected ways. Lead them down one path, only to switch things, or surprise them.

Before we get into details – part of this embracing of your powers and desires for emotional manipulation involves a bit of self-awareness. You know how people, screenwriting gurus and books keep saying things like "write the movie/TV series you want to see?" Which is solid, if incredibly simplistic advice. But hey, let's go with it. Before you write your scenes, think about how you like to be made to feel when you watch something. Do you like to be mildly confused, say something like the original season of *True Detective* (please don't watch season 2, you'll only get disheartened, or do watch it from the perspective of learning what NOT to do in pretty much every scene), or the movie *The Arrival*? Or do you like to be shocked and scared, or feel a slow burn of emotions that end up boiling over later? Or do you like to laugh at characters falling down, or being humiliated, or being witty and smart? Sacha Baron Cohen and my friend Ant Hines (a writer on *Borat*) love finding the humor in making people uncomfortable. I mention that because they are clear on the type of humor they want to explore and deliver for an audience who loves cringing and laughing. They know exactly what they are trying to achieve before they do anything.

Have a think about who you are as an audience member. How do you watch your entertainment? Do you turn your brain off, and just roll with whatever you're watching? Or are you like most of us, and always trying to stay one step ahead of whatever you are seeing?

Side note here – if you answered that last question with "I just go with the flow" then you need to not be like that as you write. The very worst thing you want to have happen as a writer is allowing the audience to get ahead of you, the characters, and the story. Remember, it's your job to entertain, and most of us enjoy watching something where we don't know exactly what's going to happen next.

I know you've watched something and groaned because there are no surprises, no twists, just boring cliché after boring cliché, so why would you write something like that? Even if you're writing a Hallmark Channel Christmas movie, there are always opportunities to deepen the level of entertainment and not settle for cliches. Always.

Really think about how you like to be entertained, and always keep an eye on your own script, to make sure it's delivering at a level you would expect from something you watch.

Now, once you've done that, it's time to mess with your audience in every way possible.

Everything that goes into your pages, can and should be used as a manipulation tool – from your first line of scene description, where you are establishing the tone and style of imagery you want strangers to experience. Then everything that follows.

Remember, your audience knows nothing about your story. Apart from a trailer they may have seen, or reviews, but you can't worry about that.

The people reading your script know even less. At most they may have read a logline, and we all know loglines totally suck.

Which means all of these people – the audience, the industry people - are willingly and very enthusiastically giving you a great gift. It's important you know and understand what it is, and how best to make use of it.

Any and every audience member who sits down to watch anything...with the possible exception of losers who go to comedy clubs to heckle on open mic nights...is handing over control of their emotional state to the artist for the time they are in the cinema, or tuned in on the couch. Full control. It's all yours, mate.

Your audience is not only giving you permission to manipulate their emotions, they are actively encouraging such behavior. They want to feel things. They want the emotional highs and lows. They want to escape from their lives for a moment, and ride someone else's story and emotional journey. It's really the only reason they are there!

Let that sink in a moment. You, as a writer, have complete control over other people's emotions, and you didn't even have to ask for it. I told you it's a great gift. Something to treasure and exploit, and yet you would be SHOCKED at how many writers fail to notice or take advantage of this treat.

Your audience wants you to mess with them, just like you want to be messed with when you are in the audience. So make every scene and every line of dialogue give them what they want.

I could bore you now with a bunch of technobabble that makes it sound like manipulating your audience requires a high degree of technical skill. But that's just demoralizing and not necessarily true. Sure – there are some truly gifted filmmakers and writers who are better at it than others. I won't mention names because we all have our favorites. Although Alfred Hitchcock is someone I would take the time to study. Say what you want about him as a human being, but as a filmmaker, he was always aware of the audience experience, and always trying to deliver something unexpected, surprising and affecting in multiple ways, not simply with story.

Phoebe Waller-Bridge, creator of "Fleabag" is another example, and my personal favorite. Okay, so I guess I am mentioning names.

I'm going to give you an example of a scene in "Fleabag" that demonstrates what I'm saying in this chapter. But let me lay out the objective first.

Your job, as a writer/entertainer, is to find ways to engage with your audience so they will love you and more people will pay you to create more content. Not only should every scene, every scene description, every character, and every line of dialogue exist with the goal of being entertaining, there is also one simple tip to immediately set you off on this manipulation goal.

Yes, I said *one tip*. And yes, it's kinda simple.

As you write your outline (I've mentioned how you really should be writing an outline, right?), you will include scenes. And within these scenes, you have figured out what information you want to convey to your audience, what you want them to know, and how you want them to feel, right? Because if you haven't figured that out, then what the hell is that scene doing in your project? I'll tell you, it's probably providing some boring logistical moment you think the audience needs to know, when we really don't.

That's a side tip – if the audience would be fine if that scene wasn't in your script, then that scene doesn't need to be in your script. Same with dialogue. I digress. Again.

Let's assume you've figured out what you want to reveal in your scene, and what you want your audience to feel. Well done! Now – here's the tip.

Take a moment with that scene. Figure out the "easy" way to write it. The straightforward, linear approach, where everything is laid out, and we move onto the next scene. Then, turn it all on its head. Try thinking about ways to subvert your "easy" way – whilst still delivering the required information. How can you make it more engaging, more unexpected, more unpredictable, without moving away from your intended goal of the scene? What little, or big things can you do to lead the audience down one path, only to switch it up on them? To play with, exploit – and yes, manipulate – their expectations so you can deliver a bigger impact.

This is something Ms. Waller-Bridge did brilliantly in her TV series. One scene in particular resonates with me. It's in the last episode of season 1. Phoebe's character has been sleeping with this guy – and after the last time, he seemed to have some sort of emotional epiphany. Fleabag interpreted that as him having some genuine feelings. The relationship was moving to a new phase potentially, and she took a moment to think about that. While she wasn't entirely on board with getting too serious, she came to the conclusion she was willing to explore the possibilities.

The man came to her stepmum's "Sexhibition," and asked to speak with her privately – outside. He began the conversation with compliments, telling her what a profound experience it was the last time they had sex, and how it had led to personal revelations, most importantly, that he realized he is in love and he doesn't want to have sex with anyone else. Now at this point in the scene, Phoebe the writer has the audience well and truly comfortable with where this conversation was heading. She even looks to the camera and says, "Here we go." The only mystery was how "Fleabag" the character would react to what we all know is coming, and how she might potentially mess this up or make it awkward, as is her way. Phoebe the writer has manipulated audience expectations, and allowed you to think you know where this is going.

And then he continues, saying his epiphany made him realize he wants to stay faithful to his girlfriend. He's done with sleeping around behind her back, and it's time to really focus on one relationship. He's so grateful to "Fleabag" for helping him reach this conclusion, and he wishes her all the best. And he's glad she doesn't care. At which point a clearly hurt woman agrees that she doesn't care.

What we all thought was a "let's get serious" chat, became a breakup chat in a matter of moments.

Now writer Phoebe could've written that scene with the man taking her outside, telling her he has a girlfriend, apologizing for not telling her sooner, saying he's decided to be faithful to her, and wishing her all the best. The scene still would've conveyed the same information, and I'm sure there would've been some jokes in there that would've made it entertaining, and bittersweet/surprising. No one would've complained. But she didn't do that. She figured out what she wanted to have happen in that scene, and then thought about ways of delivering that information in surprising, and unexpected ways. In other words, she willingly manipulated our expectations and emotions, and made that scene considerably more entertaining and impactful. And all she needed to do was give it a little more thought. From the perspective of "how can I make this more entertaining for the audience, make the most of the moment, and fully exploit their expectations?"

I've no doubt Phoebe's background in theatre helped. In my limited experience (directing one play) and my years in the writing workshop, I definitely and entirely support the idea that the more you hear your words out loud, and the more often you can see, hear and feel an audience's reaction, the better your manipulation skills will be. But as it's not that easy to throw together a play, or staged reading, I don't want you thinking you can't grow these skills without that step. You can. You definitely can. But if you feel like putting together a reading, it will never be a waste of time. Ever. Even if Grandma really can't pull off the role of "super villain."

It's also worth noting Phoebe's years in the theatre only pay off if she's willing and able to listen, learn, and use that experience. To listen to the impact her words have on strangers. To learn how to maximize their emotional experience. To be aware of the power we writers really and truly have.

If you give every scene in your script that level of extra thought – and never lose sight of your manipulation powers - you won't change your story, you won't upset your characters, but you will write a far more compelling script. And you will show readers that you have thought about your audience and are in solid command of your craft.

Easy, right? Every scene. Every line of dialogue. How can I make this more entertaining, and how can I subvert and manipulate the expectations of my audience?

Manipulation – in this context – is not only a good word – it's really a crucial word. The more you can do it, the more your audience will enjoy your script/movie/TV pilot.

But I do have one, small warning.

Don't get too crazy, and veer into making choices that are unrealistic for the characters, or the tone you are trying to achieve. This is not a power to be abused. Sure, it might be tempting in the middle of your searing historical romance to throw in an alien, or a vampire – but that's not manipulation. That's shock value. That's going for cheap thrills. Tone always comes first. Be clear about what you are writing, and keep your manipulative skills within those boundaries.

Let me summarize all this in a reassuring way. I'm pretty sure, at some point in your life, you have organized a surprise for someone. Could be a party, a gift, flowers, some travel, a dinner, something you set up that the person you are intending to surprise is not aware of. Hopefully you've done that. If you haven't – please go do it now. Surprising someone by organizing something lovely for them makes everyone feel good, right? The surprise element adds an extra layer of enjoyment for your intended target. In the moment where all is revealed, they feel seen, taken care of, and appreciated. That someone has taken the time to organize something just for them, purely because they knew it would be enjoyable, is something we should all be doing to each other all the time. It's not hard.

But sometimes it requires preparation, even convincing the person that what will happen is definitely not happening. We do this so the surprise can not only be kept secret, but actually amplified. You lead the person in one direction, only to reveal the switch, and that makes the whole event even more fun, and awesome. It's like the emotional response has been amplified because the person didn't see it coming.

See where I'm going here? If you know how good it feels for someone to have their emotions manipulated when joy is the goal in real life, why wouldn't you apply all of that to your script? And what's more fun, in the script, joy doesn't have to be the goal! You can surprise with murder, betrayal, violence, love, humor, whatever you want. In the script. In real life, maybe stick to joy and love. Makes everything easier.

If you've had those good feelings in your life when you've led someone down a wrong path, only to see the look on their face and feel the love in their heart when the truth is revealed, then you know the power of manipulation, and you can apply it in your script. Constantly.

Keep in mind how much more fun it is when someone discovers something they did not expect. Use that power in your writing. All it takes is an understanding of what information you want your scene to contain, and then thinking about ways to deliver that information in unexpected ways. Remember, I'm not talking about constant plot twists. I'm talking about thinking more about how you deliver the plot and characters you want to explore. So don't stress about needing some piano crashing from the ceiling in every scene. Or any scene really.

Time for another quick writing exercise. Have a look at something you've written, and focus on one scene where some important piece of information is revealed. Take a moment to look at the scene, and on a notepad or laptop or phone, jot down a few ways that scene could deliver the required information, in a different way/order/rhythm. Give yourself some options. Think wildly outside the box. Just one scene, no need to go crazy. I'm confident something will pop into your head that has never popped in there before. It may be entirely stupid – but new ideas and thoughts are never entirely a waste of time, right?

One way to take command of an audience's emotional experience is to harness your own emotional experiences and vulnerabilities. Which I would argue is one of, if not the hardest aspect of writing. So obviously we must explore that now!

8

---·---

WHY FEELING
UNCOMFORTABLE MATTERS

This is the chapter where things get a little messy. Where you may feel a little uncomfortable. And where you may want to fight me. I understand. We're heading off into territory you may not want to explore. We're going to discuss things you probably didn't think you would need to discuss when you developed the fantasy of being a globally praised, Oscar winning, box office dominating screenwriter. Oh well. It's not going to stop me going there. But by now you know that about me.

You, yes you, have a unique, and rich emotional history. Even if you don't think you do. You have lived a life no one else has lived. I am raising twin girls, who at the time of writing are teenagers. They've spent pretty much their entire lives together, having similar life experiences, and yet they are vastly different human beings, with vastly different emotional lives. No one, not one single person on this planet, sees and experiences the world exactly the way you do. No one, not one single person on this planet has

111

exactly the same emotional responses to life experiences. Which means no one – not one single person on this planet – will write a screenplay exactly the same way you will.

Side note: Those last few sentences were a call back to my earlier comments about being afraid to tell a stranger your story idea out of concern they may steal it. Even if someone does decide to grab your basic premise about a sponge who wants to destroy the earth, there is zero chance they will write the same script as you. Zero. Oh sure, there might be some similar scenes, probably involving a sponge. But they won't write your script, just like you could never hope to write theirs. So let me say again, when you meet someone remotely related to the industry who asks for more info when you tell them you're writing a script, tell them about the script. Please.

Okay, back to the topic of the chapter. Which is exploring your emotional history, and how you can use that valuable and unique resource to give your script that extra, magic pixie dust to elevate it from the pack.

First, your emotional history probably has a wide range of stuff. Good, fun, awesome, sad, awful, painful, and everything in between. All of those feelings are useful. If I may use a building analogy for a moment – if you think of your script as a home under construction, your warehouse of emotional experiences and feelings are the accents that makes the house a home. It's what shifts the new construction from a cold, dull, well-constructed establishment, into a rich, vibrant, engaging living space.

As I may have mentioned on pretty much every page of this book, your goal is not to simply build the cold, well-constructed generic house. Your job is to create a welcoming home, a safe space for your audience to feel all the feels, to engage in a rich emotional experience.

Obviously your home needs to be structurally sound. But if your idea of a great home is something that has four walls, a roof, some windows, doesn't leak when it rains, and nothing else...then your home will not earn top dollar with buyers, or frankly with anyone who comes to visit. It will be sterile. Nicely built, and you'll get compliments about the construction skill. People will say "Gosh, that looks and feels like a house. Not a house I would ever want to live in, but I can't deny it's a well-made house."

What you aim to do is fill your well-constructed house with all the stuff that converts it into a home. What would that stuff be? What would you add to a house to make it a home? I'm starting to think I could ride this analogy for a lot longer than I first thought.

The best homes reflect the emotional life of the occupant. Their deeply held likes and dislikes. The dislikes manifest in what is absent from the home (just like great dialogue can often be about what is not said). Their mementos from travel, or reminders of family, or times in their life they wish to remember. Even the things that matter most to them...maybe it's an artist, maybe it's a couch, maybe it's sports team memorabilia. A home also reflects the personal taste of the occupant. From the choice of counter top, to wall colors, to throw pillows, and even the size of the TV.

Your home reflects who you are. Your screenplay really should serve the same purpose. With less throw pillows.

You know when you visit a friend's house – and I promise I'm leaving this analogy behind soon – and you see a pic of a relative who has died – what do you think? You probably don't think "Oh, how gross, displaying the pic of someone who means something to them who is no longer here. They are shoving their sadness or fondness for the deceased down my throat. Terrible." Right? If you do think that, then I don't mind saying you are not in a healthy mindset.

No, of course you don't think that. You see the pic, you probably ask who they are, and you nod and say "I'm sorry for your loss," when they tell you how important that person is, and how much they are missed. Or you laugh when they tell you the funny anecdote that goes with that specific photo.

Now, if your friend has built a whole freaking shrine in the living room, and covered the walls with photos both nice and weird, and spent the entire time talking about that deceased loved one, drowning out every other conversation – you might use the words "heavy handed." But you certainly get their grief, and their emotional state.

The same, again, applies to your script. Infusing it with your unique emotional experience makes it entirely more interesting. We humans like to explore other people's emotional experiences. We like to listen and learn, and mostly compare it with our own experiences. It's how we connect as people. It's always been how we connect as people. You think ancient cave paintings showing people being chased by buffaloes, or just a simple hand print isn't trying to connect us as a tribe, a people, a species?

Connection is what sustains us. Think about all the emotional experiences on the palette of life. Right up there with sadness and pain is...loneliness. No one likes to be lonely. Which is different from wanting to be alone. Loneliness sucks. We go to amazing lengths to fight against it. From social media (which I'm not convinced does the job we think it does), to improv comedy classes, to bird watching groups, to brothels. To going to movies so we can feel a part of the human experience. We can spend two hours (please, no more three-hour movies), immersed in the emotional experiences of characters we will never meet...because they don't exist in the real world. But for the time we spend with them, they feel very much alive, and very much connected to us on an emotional level. We actually care what happens to them. We worry for them, we are scared for them, we are sad and happy for them. These people who do not exist.

Such is our desire for and love of human connection.

How cool is that?

And yet most of the scripts I read from unsigned writers either downplay this, or ignore it completely – preferring to focus on not making the roof leak. Okay, that was the last house analogy reference I promise.

Why is that you ask? If human connection and our emotional experience is so valuable, so enriching, and so important in storytelling, why is it so often under-explored?

Because it's hard.

Much harder than reading a book, following a template, and ticking all the "action on this page" boxes. Why is it harder? Surely if we're all unique emotional creatures with a deeply held desire to connect and a deeply held hatred of loneliness, infusing our stories with an emotional core should be easy. You're right, it probably should be. And yet, it's not.

Here's why I think it's so hard. Just like earlier when I mentioned the big reason writers stuff their opening pages with all the backstory and character development we don't actually need, the big reason many scripts are emotionally dry is...

Fear.

This fear is way worse than the other one. Because here we're talking about inviting strangers into our emotional dark places. The rooms inside us that hold the strongest emotional responses. The stuff that makes us cry, or laugh, or love, or hate. The rooms where our passions live. Who wouldn't be uncomfortable putting stuff in their script that leaves them feeling vulnerable, and exposed? Every writer battles with that – because they are human. But the great writers do it anyway. They know, the only way to break through to an audience is to be as fully exposed and vulnerable as they can be within the context of the story they want to tell. The ONLY WAY.

The challenge is basically to challenge yourself. To be willing to have a look at the story you want to tell, and find ways to inject it with authentic emotional experiences for the characters, and the audience. Which means digging into your warehouse of authentic emotional experiences. Which is hard, and sucks.

As I have mentioned throughout this book, the advice here applies to all genres – even comedy and horror. The more authentic you make the characters and their emotional journeys, the more compelling your script will be to strangers. You will connect us to your characters.

One film that sticks out for me is *Happy Gilmore*, an Adam Sandler movie that features every kind of stupid antic you would imagine. It's a broad comedy aimed at teenagers and those of us who think like teenagers. It would be easy to just write it off as a movie with a lot of slapstick and silly humor, which Adam Sandler did better than just about anyone. But Sandler's character is doing everything he can to save his grandmother's house from being taken away from her. Sure, it's a handy plot device, but it becomes obvious early enough in the script that this relationship means a lot to Happy. And as the story progresses, Happy's emotional journey begins. He grows emotionally and becomes more capable of having a more adult-style relationship with a woman and a stronger understanding of the people in his life and what they really mean to him. He is not the same stupid, juvenile, angry man-child he is at the beginning of the movie.

Argue all you want about the reasons for that film's success. But if you take a moment to look at the central character's emotional journey – it's there – and it comes with emotional vulnerability. Happy's future successes depends on him being willing to be more emotionally vulnerable. When I say this stuff applies to every genre, I mean it!

So how do you dig into your emotional stuff? How do you figure out just how vulnerable to be, and how do you fight that feeling that once everyone knows your deepest, darkest secrets they won't look at you the same way again. In other words, they'll judge you, and you'll be exposed, and ruined as a human being.

Let's take all that one step at a time. First – how do you figure out what to share and what not to share? The easy answer would be to just share everything. Don't hold back. If your story demands it, put it in. But that's too simple, and can lead to some oversharing, which could get awkward, and send your script off track.

Instead – it's what I mentioned earlier. Take a moment to figure out what is drawing you to this particular idea, at this particular time in your life. What are the underlying themes of the story you want to tell? What do you keep coming back too as you think about your idea, and your characters, as you write notes for your outline?

We are all evolving creatures emotionally. And we all have things that are more present at certain times of our life. I'm willing to bet whatever idea is floating your boat right now, has some connection to what's going on in your emotional life. Hopefully anyway. The challenge is, it may not be obvious at first glance.

And even if it's not super obvious – then you have an opportunity to think about your characters and their journeys, and see if there's a way to line them up with where you head is currently at.

I saw a video interview with Quentin Tarantino once, where he said it didn't matter what script he was writing, if he wasn't including some aspect of his current emotional state, then he wasn't doing the script, or himself justice. If he's going through a breakup and he's writing a World War II prisoner escape movie, there's still a way to infuse the script with his authentic emotional state.

Look at it this way – you are a human, and you are at a point in your life's journey right now, that you will never be again. With that comes a boatload of emotional opportunities. You can be most honest, authentic and vulnerable with the place you are right now. It's the low-hanging fruit on the emotional spectrum really. It's the whole "write what you know" thing. So why not use it? Why not take advantage of this wonderful opportunity?

There are so many advantages to making the most of your current place in life, and finding ways to infuse some of your thoughts, feelings and emotions into your work. Let me share one example from my own writing life.

When I was 22, as mentioned earlier, I was hired to write some episodes of the TV series "*Neighbours*". I had a day job, it was overwhelming and all that. One of the episodes I was writing had a moment where the character being played by Guy Pearce was explaining to a woman why he didn't want to get tied down in a relationship. As a writer on the show, you are sent an episode breakdown, where every scene is explained – as in "Joe walks in, catches Mary smoking, and he's angry" – and then the writer adds the dialogue and fleshes it all out. The production wants you to use some of your own creativity to elevate the dull sentences they send you.

I was 22 and six months into a full time job as a TV News producer/journalist – first time living on my own, first time working in live television, first time handling the responsibilities of a full time job, and then a second job writing for a hugely successful international soap opera. I was also coaching an under 8 soccer team. To say life was full would be an understatement.

At the time, I had a huge crush on our news anchor. She was smart, not much older than me, and when we were alone we got along really well. When we were in a group, she reverted to being a TV "star." She was young and her face was on the sides of buses in Canberra – the capital city of Australia (no, it's not Sydney), but a relatively small town – so I totally got the attitude, even if it frustrated young me.

One day, when we were alone, we had a discussion about the possibility of us actually, maybe, trying to have some sort of relationship. It may have been less discussion, and more me politely asking if something was going to happen or not. At that point I was pretty confused and eager for clarity.

The news anchor then gave me a speech – in darkness, outside the home she was sharing with two roommates who became my friends too. It was a warm evening, and I will always remember her speech about her not being in a place where she wanted to be "tied down." And how we were young, she had a lot going on, I was awesome, but her head space just wasn't thinking about a relationship. I don't think she actually said "It's not you, it's me," but that was the gist. She was honest, a little egocentric, and she made her point clearly and somewhat brutally. But at least I was left in no doubt.

I went home, a bit deflated. And annoyed. So when the "Neighbours" episode outline arrived soon after (in the mail – it was a long time ago), and I saw the Guy Pearce scene – I pretty much wrote him the exact speech I'd recently been given by my anchor friend.

The producers loved it – praised my efforts, didn't change a word, and a few weeks later, I watched Guy Pearce deliver the speech to the female character who wanted to date him. Me, and 40 million other people worldwide got to enjoy a moment of genuine authenticity from a character in a soap opera. The news anchor never knew a thing about it, or at least she never mentioned it to me. I don't think she watched the episode, and even if she did, there's no way she would've joined the dots.

I could've written Guy's little monologue a hundred different ways. But I chose the most authentic way. It was where my head was at, it was a fresh emotional experience for me, and one of the skills and perks of being a writer is the ability to remember stuff, and spit it back out when the time comes. Why waste time trying to manufacture artificial emotions?

As you build your characters, think about their emotional truths. Your emotional truths. What is in your head and your heart right now? How can you use all that great stuff in your script, rather than spending lots of time trying to come up with different emotional journeys?

I'm not saying re-create actual stories from your past. I want to be clear. I'm talking about finding ways to insert your emotional authenticity into whatever story you want to tell, not diving into your grab bag of personal tales about that time you took a road trip to the Grand Canyon or when you discovered they had crunchy peanut butter as well as smooth. It's an important distinction.

Guy Pearce's character was not an idiot 22-year-old living in Canberra coaching soccer and balancing too many jobs. He was a character in a soap opera. Still, I was able to give that character a moment of emotional authenticity thanks to my willingness to explore what I was feeling, and finding a way to fit it into his soap opera character's world. That difference is important. Our regular lives are usually pretty dull. Our emotional lives...less so.

Your job is to make us feel stuff. To care about the characters in your story. To connect with them on some level that isn't story related. The more we can understand them, feel for them, feel anything really, the better your script will be. And the more authentic you can make these characters and their journeys, the easier they will be to write on some levels. Of course, writing will be harder on other levels, because you should be dipping into your emotional messy bits. But it will definitely give strangers an easier time understanding the decisions your characters make in your story.

That's really a win/win for you. All you have to do is take a deep breath, be brave, and access your emotional world.

How do you know if you've got it right? Or at least made yourself and your characters a little emotionally vulnerable? I've got a handy answer to that question.

First, do your best to make yourself uncomfortable. As you are writing a scene, either in the outline or the draft, you want to have moments where you ask "Should I really put that in?"

Deliberately seek out that awkward feeling you're maybe cutting a little close to the bone for you on a personal and emotional level.

Handy tip #1 – Every single time you find yourself asking that question, make sure the answer is an immediate yes. Getting to that point is a victory to be celebrated. Asking that question means you are in the right place, delving into the right emotional options for your characters. Never second guess that, always dig deeper.

Handy tip #2 – When your draft is done, show it to people. Before you hit send on the email, or hand over the printed copy if you still do that – take a moment for yourself. Check in with your feelings. Hopefully, alongside all the usual insecurities, self-doubt and imposter syndrome garbage we all deal with constantly, there will be another little voice whispering. He, she or it will be asking if you're going to make a fool of yourself. If you're revealing too much. Maybe there's a small cold sweat, and a little existential dread that you will be exposed for having all these thoughts and feelings, and you will never be able to talk to that person again once they read your script. This could be it for that relationship. Obviously, that's just a stupid voice, and your relationship will be fine. Maybe even stronger.

But you want that voice. You want that moment of dread, the worry that you may have gone too far and injected too much of you in this draft.

When I was a member of that writing lab I mentioned earlier and actors would read portions of my script in front of my peers, I quickly discovered that when I was presenting pages that made my hands go cold (how I deal with stress) and my stomach got tight and uncomfortable, I was more likely to have a genuinely good reading. If I didn't have those pre-game nerves in that particular way, chances are my script was going to be pleasant, enjoyable, but wouldn't connect with the crowd. So I started to focus on giving myself those feelings. Making myself feel like I was being too open with my thoughts and feelings. And you know what? My scripts got better. Fast.

I went from being the cute and occasionally funny writer, to someone able to give my audience a genuine emotional experience.

Remember – again – your audience wants to *feel*. Your audience wants to *connect*. It's a huge part of being human. If you hold your script at arm's length from your current, personal emotional state, you will hold the audience at arm's length, and your script will not connect, and it will not succeed.

I wish I had a template for you. I wish I could give you tips on how to access how you're feeling. I can't.

But I do have a metaphor!

Imagine your genuine emotional vulnerability – the truly impactful feelings you have – are at the bottom of a well. To write a compelling script, you have to find a way down into that well. Too many unsigned writers spend their scripts circling the well. I can feel it as I read. There are issues they want to explore, they get to the edge of the well, they peek tentatively over the edge, and then slowly back away. Those are the moments that define a script and a writer.

So instead of a handy template, just jump into the well. If you feel yourself getting a little tentative, try to push through it. Understand those moments really are everything in a script. Don't circle the well. Find the courage and jump in! It's the best way to connect us to your story, and connection in storytelling is everything. Everything.

Here's another little exercise to try. Take a moment to think about your characters, and what you want them to do in your story. Try to figure out – using words you write down – the feelings they are grappling with. Or the feelings you want them to grapple with. Come up with a list of emotions. Not just words like "scared," but next level. Stuff like "afraid they'll never be loved," or "angry they never got the respect they deserved." You'll be amazed not only how much better and more quickly you get to know your people, but also, hopefully, you'll quickly realize how much their struggles or issues resonate with you.

Connection is everything. Between you and your script, you and your characters, and you and your audience.

9

TEMPERATURE CHECKS

Now you have faced all of your fears, delved deeply into your emotional tool box, given your characters all sorts of genuinely human qualities and active decisions to make, it's time to confront another issue that regularly afflicts screenplays I read. Don't worry, the list of afflictions is shortening – you can see how long this book is, so there aren't many to go.

Temperature checks. Or should I say, a lack of them. What am I talking about?

One of the side effects of our recent obsession with "story," and the teachings of grouchy old guru Robert McKee, is a tendency from unsigned writers to put all their eggs in that basket. "Story is King/Queen! Viva La Story! Story, Story, Story, Oy, Oy, Oy!" I threw that last one in to celebrate my Aussie roots. My point is, when you get bombarded with the importance of story, there is a tendency to focus on it at the expense of everything else.

I've touched on many of the things that get overlooked, and temperature checks are as important as anything else. I'll explain what I mean, but first, let me give you a little example.

I read some feedback recently on a script I have not read. The feedback was well thought out, helpful, useful, considered, and smart. And it was entirely focused on points and story beats. The script was apparently a thriller, and all the very helpful feedback was aimed at making the script more thrilling. Awesome, right? Kinda.

Just reading the feedback, I was left wondering about the central character. Sure, they are immersed in uncovering some sort of truth, and I guess avoiding getting killed in the process. But I got no real sense of who this person was, and what they wanted. Why were they devoting so much time and energy and possible death, to solve this thrilling puzzle? What was in it for them? And how was this puzzle changing them? Was it impacting them on any kind of emotional level? Forcing them to rethink what they thought they knew about themselves, and the world around them?

My point? Not only are writers brainwashed into story, story, story, but even the people helping writers improve their skills are re-enforcing the "story at all costs" approach. What we end up with is a potentially awesome story, filled with cardboard cut-out characters that we, the audience, never really get to know, and therefore never really get to care about, which means the thrilling script is no longer thrilling. All the potential twists and turns are dull because they are happening to or involving people we simply don't care about.

How many times have you found yourself being told a story by a friend/loved one about someone you don't know, who has stuff happen to them, and you find yourself nodding and making all the right facial expressions, while internally wondering what to have for dinner? Maybe you get engaged because you love the storyteller, or maybe that storyteller is really freaking good at telling an ultimately meaningless story. But you're never fully engaged. Right? Dinner thoughts remain.

Temperature checks. Taking time out of your story obsession to give the audience a little visit with the central characters – to see how the story they are in is impacting them as a human being. How the story is impacting what they thought they wanted when we first met them. A pause. A moment or two. An aside. A temperature check. Taking the emotional temperature of the humans/sponges populating your story.

How do they feel about killing someone? How do they feel about seeing a dead body? How do they feel about the new information they have discovered about someone they love? Or someone they thought they hated? Or how they are handling the obstacles they are facing? Are they scared? Worried? Excited? Grappling with their own emotional stubbornness? Resisting these new feelings they are having? Worried about what's in the basement? Wondering if they can trust the new people they just met in a prison in space? Grappling with the idea that the leader of the Empire might be their father? Wondering how to cope with a world no longer dominated by women but now seemingly run by Kens?

Temperature checks. Sounds easy, yet rarely inserted into scripts by unsigned writers who believe they have to keep their foot on the story pedal at all costs, or risk certain and immediate death.

Why are they so important?

This entire book is built around the relationship you, the writer, has with the audience of strangers. Your script is an on-going communication with them – every scene, every word in every scene. Sometimes the communication is purely story based, sometimes purely character information, sometimes a combination. With that context, part of the communication really should involve the development of the characters, based on what's been going on.

Before I continue, I should point out one of the foundations of screenwriting. Sorry it's taken me this long to mention it. Every scene in your script only needs to do one of two things. It either moves the story along, or it reveals something new about a character...or possibly both. That's it. If it's not doing either of those things, you can safely cut it. Remember, something NEW about a character. Or a new twist on something we already know. Avoid repetition. I repeat, avoid repetition.

Okay – so assuming your job is to entertain (as we've established) and connecting these strangers to your characters is a major way to achieve that entertainment – then the temperature checks are invaluable. They give your audience a chance to catch their breath, and check in with the characters they now find themselves caring about.

Here's an example from the car racing movie based on the video game *Grand Turismo*.

Yep – it's a movie based on a driving simulation game, about Nissan sponsoring an attempt to get someone obsessed with the video game to become an actual race car driver, in an actual racing car.

The movie hits all the story notes you expect. The kid wants to be a driver, he gets an opportunity, everyone thinks it's crazy, he keeps dramatically winning and progressing etc. It even has a family life where his Dad would prefer he get a real job, and give up his fanciful/stupid dreams of driving real, expensive race cars.

Now this is a movie paid for by a video game and a car company. It could've easily focused all its energy on driving related stuff. The video game does that, right? It doesn't take time out to give us backstories...or emotional growth...it gives us cars to drive and fantasies to indulge.

Right before the big, final, climactic race, the kid star – now an actual car driver – gets a surprise visit from his Dad. It's a small, quiet scene, in a trailer. Dad hugs his kid, and bursts into tears – telling his son he understands he wasn't supportive enough, and he feels terrible about that. And he tells his son he is insanely proud of what he has achieved, against all the odds. His son tells his Dad how proud he is to be his son, and how he's doing this for him. These two men share hugs, and tears, and it's a surprisingly moving moment for anyone who has a kid...like me.

This scene doesn't add anything to the race car driving momentum. It doesn't even build stakes – like say Russell Crowe getting stabbed by Joaquin Phoenix right before his final battle in "Gladiator." But it's a powerful moment – because it's a temperature check.

It's a quiet moment before the climax, where we, the audience, get a chance to see how all of what we have seen and experienced has impacted a profound relationship to both of these characters. The son gets to understand where his Dad's head is at, and Dad gets to feel less guilty, and also understand how much his son loves and cares about him. The whole scene takes about two minutes. But it's important in terms of connecting us with the characters. Having a moment to catch our breath, and see how the story has impacted our central characters matters. It connects us with the characters in ways pure story will never be able to do.

We've all seen movies and TV where these scenes don't happen. And I've read plenty of scripts that avoid this stuff like it's somehow infected with some plague. We walk away from these pieces of entertainment saying "That was fun, what's for dinner?" Or "That was overwhelming, what's for dinner?" Or "That was crap, what's for dinner?"

We've also seen movies where the temperature checks are used. There's a reason soldiers tell each other about the girl they are looking forward to seeing when they get home, or how scared they are, right before they leap out of the trench into machine gun fire. The writer is giving you, the audience member, a moment to connect with this person before they face almost certain death. It helps you care, and gives you someone to root for because you are now more aware of the stakes and how they are feeling.

Small, quiet, character-based moments matter, way more than you think they do. Way more.

So why are they largely absent from so many scripts I read? Are you ready? I'm going to give you that word again. Yep...

Fear.

Who knew screenwriting was so connected with our deepest fears? Me. Because I've been writing for years and have been forced to confront them all.

This fear actually isn't deep and dark, to be fair. It's entirely connected with the "story is king/queen" obsession.

Many unsigned writers fear if they slow the pace of their script, even for a moment, they'll bore the audience, who will get distracted, lose interest, and walk out, change the channel/streamer or put the script down.

Remember that industry advice "make every page compelling?" Yeah, that's damaging, because it makes assumptions on the definition of "compelling." A lot of readers/industry folk and writers think "compelling" means strong story beats. Something shocking, or eventful, or dramatic, or wild, or fascinating, or surprising. You get the idea. Compelling equals action baby!

Let's throw that advice where it belongs. Or...be brave enough to expand the definition. I'd prefer you just chuck it out because it's overly simplistic and far too easy to misinterpret.

Fear of boring your audience has a lot of power, and it's easy to justify in this context. If you feel the pressure to impress an industry reader, your natural inclination is to think of ways to stuff your script with amazing stunts, or shocks, or visual imagery, or blah blah blah. I mean, even I say your first ten pages has to show what you can do, or a reader will stop reading. Surely that means all your best adventures as quickly, and constantly as you can. No, it doesn't mean that. But I understand the confusion.

Seeing a character be vulnerable, or grappling with a tough decision, or trying to come to terms with what's going on, has power. Being brave enough to write a scene that basically takes a timeout from the story, so you can bring the audience up to speed with how your central characters are doing has power. But it requires courage to execute.

Let me reassure you. Take it from me – someone who has launched writing careers and who has read more scripts than you've had hot dinners – stepping out of your story to check in on the emotional state of your people is not boring. It's useful, it can be truly powerful, and it makes the difference between a good script, and a dull script. You wouldn't find it boring as a viewer, right?

Remember, many industry people I've spoken with skim action sequences to see if someone important has died. Whatever insane stunt you've imagined holds less power than a character fighting their fears, or realizing what they thought they wanted has been overwhelmed by new feelings, or new information, based on the journey you've put them on.

Honestly, if a writer wrote "insert crazy stunt here where the villain gets injured" instead of a page long series of camera cues and specific fight moves or car turns or whatever...I would be okay, and the script would not genuinely suffer. I mean, I might think the writer was a little lazy, but you get the point. Please don't start doing that in your script.

There's a reason the *Fast and the Furious* franchise has earned billions and mentions the word "family" more times than a drinking game can tolerate. Crazy stunts have their place...but without the emotional foundation, they don't create a franchise. Emotional foundations are built on small, regular temperature checks.

Before we move on, remember this important aspect of screen-writing. Everything you write focuses on the emotional journey of your central characters. Who they are when we meet them at the beginning of your script is not who they are at the end. That's the aim, the goal, the intent, the everything. If your characters go through your story, then can simply go home, resume life as it was, unchanged by the experience, your script has very little chance of success., mostly because your story will probably be a bit boring.

Life is change. We tell stories of change. Physical, emotional, both. Regular temperature checks allow the audience to be along for the ride – change wise. If you simply introduce characters, then get lost in a world full of plot and story, and revisit these characters at the end being changed and different, you've missed an opportunity. You've not given your audience a chance to think back later at the progression of the changes. To watch not simply the conclusion of the metamorphosis of the characters, but the milestones along the way.

An easy example is in *School of Rock*. Jack Black's character is a selfish dick when we meet him – lost in his "art," unwilling to see anything else, even to the point of pretending to be his roommate/best friend so he can get a job. He even uses the kids to help him achieve his rock star dreams. Then about halfway through the script – when he takes the kids to a battle of the bands audition – one of the kids wanders off, and Jack's character goes into full protective mode. It's the first time we see him show genuine concern for someone other than himself. Dare I say it, but his character is becoming "responsible." It's the first really obvious sign that his emotional journey is having an impact. These kids are changing him. He's starting to care about other people as much, or even more than himself.

It's a small moment, but it's a temperature check. Jack's character doesn't notice, because that moment isn't there for him, it's there for us. It's there so we can see the changes, and come to appreciate Jack's character and not just laugh at how awful he is...or has been.

If you want TV examples – look me in the eye and tell me the *X-Files* worked so well because of all the alien conspiracies and not because of the complex relationship between the central characters. Tell me *Game of Thrones* was big because of dragons. Tell me any successful show is successful because of the plot versus our relationship with the characters. Then tell me these shows never take a moment to let the audience connect with these characters as their lives evolve and their feelings change.

As you plot your outline, carve out some moments for a little check in with the characters. Remind yourself rather than being "boring," they are actually vitally important moments. The connective tissue between you and your audience. Rather than worrying your audience or your reader won't be compelled, remind yourself these temperature checks actually make everything far more compelling in the ways that matter most...the audience's emotional connection with your characters.

Quiet moments matter. Like, a lot.

10

—·—

WHAT THE HELL IS YOUR "VOICE", AND HOW DOES IT RELATE TO SEX?

C hances are, if you've ever had a conversation with anyone remotely associated with the movie/TV industry, you've heard a variation of this sentence: "We're looking for an original voice." At which point, two things pop into your head. "What the hell are they talking about?" And then "Do I have it? I think I have it. Yeah, I'm sure I do. Maybe? What the hell are they talking about?"

I would like to reassure you, once and for all – the "we're looking for an original voice" advice is garbage. It's true, but it's still a stupid, simplistic, vague, wishy-washy, convenient thing to say, and is usually followed by an unhelpful explanation/definition. Often, when asked a follow up, like "What do you mean by original voice?", the well-meaning industry person will shrug, and offer a version of "we know it when we see it."…which, obviously, is even less useful than the original wisdom.

So, let's use this chapter to explore what the hell they are talking about, how it directly relates to your emotional connection with your audience, and then we'll veer into comparing the use of your voice with the way you have sex. Yes, I'm serious.

Original voice. What is it? I can tell you it is difficult to define. Which is why your industry person was so vague. If it was simple, no one would be looking for it, because it would be everywhere.

Based on my experience, and a lot of thought, here is what I have concluded is something resembling your voice, when read in a screenplay.

It's finding ways to make the script your own.

This means reminding you, again, to embrace one simple but profound aspect of our life experience on this planet. No one, not one single person, is exactly the same as you. No one sees the world exactly the way you do. No one interprets information and experiences the way you do. No one uses language exactly the way you do. No one thinks about things in quite the same way. For all we know, no one may actually see colors the way you do. (Yes, I know science has proven we see similar colors, otherwise there wouldn't be sooooo many shades of white at the paint store, but still, do we really?)

What this uniqueness means is no one can write your script exactly the way you can – but only if you are willing to make your script your own.

Most of the scripts I read lack "voice." They are generic. They may follow the story charts, or they don't. But they are often either direct rip-offs of movies or TV I've seen, or they feature characters I've seen before, or they play everything so safe, that it becomes devoid of soul. Lifeless. Lying flat on the page. No "voice."

Usually this happens because the writer is inexperienced and wants to prove they can write a movie, or the writer is lazy, and is ripping off stuff they've seen on TV, or the writer hasn't embraced what I'm talking about here. Or, it's a combination of all three.

If you finish a script and pat yourself on the back because it's a perfect demonstration of your pitch – which is that you have written a movie that's *Die Hard* meets *Die Hard 2* – then there's a good chance your script is already doomed.

I know, I know, this industry loves "comps," which is a shorthand used by busy execs and reps to convey the genre and tone of a new script in ways other busy execs and reps can understand. The whole thing where a writer needs to name two existing projects their script most closely resembles, so the mildly curious industry person can immediately get a sense of whether the script is worth any follow up questions. It's kinda like describing a food someone hasn't tried before. Good luck trying to explain "Vegemite" to Americans. It's like nothing they have tasted, and as a result, it's a really hard sell, especially when you tell them it's black, and you're supposed to spread it really thinly on toast. It's a great example of why writers don't feel encouraged to be super original with their ideas or pitches. Saying "It's the Vegemite of rom-coms" will get you nowhere.

If the person has no frame of reference, it's a harder sell. We humans like to compare. And if you can use some very successful/popular movies in your "comp," then the logic goes you increase your chances of attracting the attention of a busy person. The logic is sound. I can't argue with that. But it's also annoying. To everyone.

Here's the weird thing about "comps," and about scripts with no voice. An industry type may be intrigued by your comps. They may be looking for something in the *Ghostbusters* meets *Alien* vein. But then they (or their assistant) reads your script, and it is indeed a perfect mash up of the comps you mentioned, and they pass because it lacks an original voice. What, the actual, f*$k? You deliver exactly that they say they want, and they don't want it because it's not original enough. Because there's no "voice".

Yep, it's insane. And it happens every day. As I mentioned, delivering a script that is a delightful mashup of other scripts means delivering a script that is flat, lifeless, and devoid of soul. So the first step toward understanding what "voice" means, is finding the strength to avoid ripping off other movies. Please, take NO comfort in the idea you have included scenes an exec/manager will love because it very much mimics something that did so well in another movie. They may say they want that, but they really, truly don't.

Which means it's okay to not listen to some of what they say, because they are saying it to avoid telling you the truth. Because the truth hurts. But here it is. They are telling you about comps and voice and all that because they don't know you, you have no track record, and as a result they have no confidence you know how to write a script, and they don't want to waste their very busy time. You'd probably do the same after being bombarded by people waving around the first draft of their opus while telling you they quit their job and moved to L.A. to become a screen-writer and they are living on their life savings, which will last three months. Oh, and this opus is the only thing they've ever written. I know you think you'd always be open to new writers, but after a while you'll get worn down and overwhelmed like everyone else – not because you're a terrible person but because there is a tsunami of pretty terrible scripts and very eager writers lacking self awareness, and enough command of craft, yet still clamoring for the big break they feel they deserve.

The "comps" are merely guiderails. The missing ingredient is...you guessed it...your original voice. Making something your own. Understanding you are unique on this planet, and find-ing the bravery or confidence to attack screenwriting with that knowledge. Trusting that your version of anything, if you fully dive in and make it your own – will appeal to strangers because it is not what they would've done. It's giving them a perspective they couldn't possibly have thought of on their own, because they are not you. But it still speaks to them. They still connect to it because it's hitting themes and topics they can relate too.

I gotta tell you something. What I just described sounds easy, and fun, but it's really hard. Because it requires/demands things from you that are terrifying, and not always easy to unlock. But unlocking them is not only the entire point of this book, it's also really important for your writing success.

You can't have an original voice if you don't have a solid sense of self. Don't worry, I'm not going to veer off into a self-help book, (although maybe that's what this has been all along?) but I will say self-awareness is useful here. If only from the point of view of having a grasp on your sense of humor, or what scares you, or your thoughts on love and relationships, depending on the genre you are exploring. Remember, as I may have mentioned, you are an artist. It's your job as an artist to explore aspects of what it is to be human. If you don't have a freaking clue about what it means for you to be human, how are you going to create something compelling for strangers?

Yes, discovering your "original voice" is tied to the whole "write what you know" line. Isn't it cool how everything is kinda tying together?

Step one on the path to embracing your voice – understanding what it means, and having at least a basic understanding of what you like.

Step two – finding the courage to write something that speaks to you, and what you like, even if it isn't an exact replica of an existing movie or series. That courage is required daily. Probably minute by minute. It's too easy to write what you think people want. Pandering is in some ways hard wired into most of us. I believe a lot of us instinctually want to make others happy, right? So what's the harm in a slightly modified version of *Seinfeld* or *Star Wars*?

There's a question to ask yourself, and then we'll get to sex. If you had a choice, would you rather someone passed on your script because it was too derivative of other shows/movies, or because it was "too original"? There are two answers to this question.

The first is obvious – I don't know if anyone has rejected a script because it was too original. They may reject it because it's not well written, or doesn't fit with the genre they are currently seeking, but "too original" is not something you hear much. In my experience it's only really used when someone has delivered a 300-page script about the secret life of grass, all written in rhyming poetry, with no actual sentence structure, and with the occasional musical number. "Too original" is probably the kindest thing to say to that. I'd like to say I have never read a script like that, but I would be lying.

The second answer is more nuanced. If you are trying to sell a script to a producer who specializes in "Hallmark" movies, or low budget horror, and you put your unique spin on it, and take it out of the template their production schedules and budget demands, then your quest for originality has taken a wrong turn. Your "voice" wasn't listening to the parameters. There is still plenty of opportunity to infuse a Hallmark Channel Christmas rom-com with your signature dry wit, or nuanced characters. Just be willing to read the room too.

Those situations aside, originality will always win out.

So what makes an original voice – specifically? Great question, and hard to answer.

In some ways it's easier for me to describe what it ISN'T.

Original voice is NOT slathering literate prose into your scene description, in some vain effort to show a reader you really should be writing a novel, and you know a lot of interesting words, and groovy ways to describe furniture.

It's NOT breaking genre rules because you felt like it and thought it would be cool. It's NOT throwing in sudden character shifts because you think the shock value will outweigh the "WTF" thoughts in the audience.

Original voice is more about emotional authenticity. All that stuff I just mentioned are gimmicks. It's not original, it's not authentic, and it doesn't deliver any kind of emotional experience to an audience. "Voice" is not gimmick. Please resist gimmicks. They do you no favors.

Your unique experience is all about characters and emotion. Sure, it's fun when you include stuff you've seen or experienced, but it's even more impactful when you can infuse your script with genuine human emotion. As perceived by you – the unique individual I have mentioned several times already. The more you can stick real emotions into your script, the more organically your voice develops. Because – you know – you perceive emotions your way.

Not only does it take courage to deliver something that speaks to you, not only does it require creative risks because it's more about your experiences and less about cliches and re-treads, but it also takes courage to understand that "voice" isn't necessarily obvious. It's not the scene description drivel. It's not necessarily something a reader can point to on the page and say "See – look at this original voice bit, right here!" The voice comes through in the entire piece, in the way the writer has taken control, and gives the reader/viewer a sense they are in charge. They are able to convey they know what they're doing, they are giving the reader/viewer a confident, competent emotional experience, and all you need to do is sit back and watch or turn the pages.

Original voice – your voice – comes through when you accept total and complete responsibility for your script. It just does. Trust me on that. When you look at the genre you are exploring, and you decide not to simply rehash other stuff. When you show control, command of craft and courage – meaning a willingness to get personal on some level.

But.

There are risks here...not just that your originality will be rejected for being too original. And by the way – can I just say if someone passes on your script for that reason, and you are confident it's not a brush off because you misspelled every second word, or forgot to use proper formatting, then please let that rejection go. Some scripts don't speak to some people. Some ideas don't fit the person reading it. No biggie. If your command of craft is solid, and your emotional experience is rich and authentic, your script will find a champion. Hopefully. The point is – that's a rejection you can live with. "I didn't understand what was going on" is a rejection you need to listen too.

***

Now, to the risks. Which brings me to sex.

You may be reading this, and feeling fired up to tell "the man" to suck it, because you're going to write your movie your way. Whilst I encourage most of that thinking, I want to remind you of the whole "write what you know, but make it emotionally accessible to strangers" bit of this book – which is really the entire book.

The quest for "voice" can lead to some awful, incredibly self-indulgent scripts. Where a writer confuses "originality" and "voice" for selfish drivel that appeals to no one except the writer, their pet, and maybe their very patient Mom, partner, or best friend.

If you feel like you are at risk of leaping into the self-indulgent pool – let me give you a simple, sex based analogy to help you through those selfish times.

There are different types of sex. There is the sex you have when you are alone, and the sex stuff you engage in with others. We all like to hope we are good at sex. Part of that definition involves...no...demands... your ability to please the aforementioned "others." Right? I mean, I know personal satisfaction is enjoyable, but if your partner isn't having a good time, then you're kinda missing half the fun of sex with others, and you're a bit of a jerk. Sex really should be two people (for the sake of this argument let's stick with two), fully engaged in feeling good, and making their partner feel good. I know it sounds obvious, but I also know we've all been in situations where that is not the case, and we know how we feel afterwards. The word "used" springs to mind.

Self-pleasuring is all about you, baby. No one else in the room. No one to judge, no one to worry about, just you, your body and your imagination/other support materials and devices. Is it ultimately as satisfying as being with someone else? That's your question to answer, but I think we can all agree that if self-pleasuring was always better than being with someone else, then we'd all be at home right now by ourselves.

Solo time has its moments. It serves its purpose, but it can also be more functional than truly satisfying, because we're missing that other ingredient – connection with someone else. A participatory audience, there to give and receive right along with you. Even better if you actually care about that someone else.

Scripts are the same. Yes, I know you were wondering. If you dive headlong into "write what you know," then you risk being alone in your house/room, and self-pleasuring until you are spent, without any regard for anyone else. Your script risks becoming self-indulgent, self-pleasuring, and almost entirely inaccessible to strangers. You don't want to write that script. If you want to earn money writing. No matter how good it may feel to you, it's ultimately not as satisfying as the alternative.

Bottom line – I encourage you to pursue your voice, find your courage, delve into your emotional tool kit, and take on the challenge of being "original" because you are being emotionally authentic. I also encourage you to keep an eye on the self-pleasuring. I would love to write a book where I tell you to just go for it, audience be damned, and to fight for your creative freedom, and then mention some starving artist who eventually found success long after they died. But that's simply not the reality of the screenwriting "business". I'm trying to help you earn money while you are breathing. And the screenwriting business is a never-ending balance of originality, voice, and compromise.

Back to sex. Being skillful at self-pleasuring does not make you a master of sex with other people. Sex with others requires additional skills – like listening, less ego, respect, an open mind, and some degree of understanding about what it takes to give, not just to receive. Every single one of those skills is required to be a competent screenwriter. Every. Single. One.

I may have mentioned this stuff is hard. And you won't get it right all of the time. Which is why rewriting is so important.

Honestly, it's the ability to balance these conflicting concepts that separate the good writers from the pack. The ability to turn personal feelings and emotions into publicly accessible experiences is the real skill. A skill earned, not naturally created – a skill honed by practice, and an ongoing willingness to not only want to please strangers but also to maintain a solid sense of self. To understand the difference between self-pleasure and actual sex. To understand the difference between gimmick and authenticity when it comes to "voice." To find the courage to be exposed, vulnerable and willing to listen, learn and grow. And to gather the wisdom and experience that only comes from writing a lot, creating a lot, and learning more instinctively what works, and what is drivel.

But for now – as you begin the journey to wisdom, experience and original "voice" just remember – self pleasure is not the same as good sex, and good sex is better than self pleasure.

Your "original voice" is not about gimmicks or moments; it's about taking command of your pages, infusing your uniqueness into your story, and your characters, and leading the audience into an emotional experience.

Trust me – anyone in this industry who says they can spot an original voice when they see/read it will agree with everything I have just written. They just may not be able to articulate it in this unique, personal way. See what I did there?

11

A QUICK WORD ABOUT WHY REWRITING MATTERS

Before we end this on a wave of inspiration and hope, I wanted to say a quick word in defense/support of rewriting within the theme of emotional connection and your audience.

If you are anything like me – you have at some stage despised rewriting. You work hard on something, you finish something, and then some pinhead like me writes a chapter in a wildly entertaining and helpful book politely telling you rewriting is not only crucial and vital and important and necessary, but that it is also something you should learn to love.

What if I don't want to love it? What if I rewrote as I went along with my first draft? What if my script is already perfect? Maybe I'm just really good at first drafts, have you thought about that? Maybe I'm like a savant, or a guru, so why are you telling me to destroy my perfect gift to the world with stupid rewrites? And what are they anyway? Once I start dismantling my precious gem, it will start to look like Frankenstein's monster.

A lot of this bluster is covering quiet truths. Maybe I don't know how to make it better? Maybe someone's notes have sown seeds of doubt, and they haven't provided any glimpse of a solution to this draft's issues? Maybe, as of this moment, I literally have no new ideas for scenes, or new directions. Maybe this is all too hard, so I'll sink or swim with my first draft.

None of that is unreasonable. All of that I have felt at one stage or another. Rewriting felt like torture for a long time for me.

And then it didn't. And then, once I rewrote a few projects a few times, I learned an important and undeniable truth. Rewriting is not some sort of addition to the writing process, some sort of annoying second phase where I turn my beautiful horse into an ugly two-headed camel based on feedback from potential morons. Oh no. I discovered rewriting is actually an essential phase of the writing process. There is no writing without rewriting. Ever.

So let's move past our rewriting worries, and embrace it. The job is not done when you type

"THE END" on the first draft. Accept it, embrace it, and lean into it.

Why is rewriting so important you ask? For a few reasons. I'll start with the biggest and most boring.

If you hold out hopes of being paid to write – you are ALWAYS going to be getting notes from people. Producers, studio execs, the director, the Russian oligarch giving you a giant check as long as his mistress is the lead, and she wants her pet poodle as a sidekick. Always.

Reject those notes, and your career slides quickly into oblivion. It actually slides into oblivion before it can be called a career.

That's the reality. If you manage to get to a position where you are a showrunner of a hit series, your notes may be minimal, or if you are Scorsese at Netflix/Apple TV, your notes maybe nonexistent – but Leonardo Di Caprio will still be making suggestions. There will still be a need to rewrite.

Embracing this phase now makes you much more employable moving forward. Embracing the rewrite now means you will have a firm command of the process, and how to integrate notes in a way that doesn't ruin everything by the time you get to the point where you have to figure out how to make a script "funnier" based on an exec's feedback.

Rewriting is the business of writing. It's unavoidable, unless you get paid to go away. You don't want to be that writer. Studios spend A LOT of money paying writers to rewrite someone else's script. A LOT of money. If you are the writer they pay to go away because you won't take notes, you are walking away from a potentially lucrative pile of cash.

But hey, if you aspire to be the writer of gritty little independent films that take fifteen years to find funding and get made, if at all, and you find joy in the struggle, and feel like no rewrite notes is a worthwhile trade-off, then I wish you every success. But I promise you, right here, right now, your gritty little movie will suck. Even those movies go through multiple drafts.

Imagine a house painter only ever doing one coat, and refusing all suggestions to fill in some spots, or maybe do another coat entirely? This is the writer refusing to do more drafts, or contemplate notes from people who pay money or who have skills and knowledge and can see blind spots in your script you may have missed.

Start practicing rewrites now. Write a draft, take a moment, then reread the draft, and be willing to acknowledge and take on the bits that aren't working. You know where they are. And you know how you feel when you read them...but you kinda skip over them so you can enjoy the really awesome next scene. Confront the ugly bits.

But rewriting can become a slippery, indecisive slope. How do we avoid going from the writer who won't change a word, to the writer who can't stop changing words, and feels like their script is never actually done? Or who gets so agreeable they start making every single change anyone and everyone suggests.

Full disclosure, I had a producer option a feature script of mine – a father/son story dealing with death and mental health. With jokes. In the first meeting after the deal, the producer asked if it could become a mother/son movie instead. Which I will argue is a fundamentally different relationship. Not better, not worse, just different dynamics. Which means a fundamentally different script.

So how do you find a balance? I have some suggestions to help.

First, let's stick with the theme of the book when discussing new drafts. Structure and story have their own challenges, and their own books addressing those challenges. So let us focus on the emotional connection with the audience and the authenticity of the characters.

Step one – Finish a first draft, then look yourself in the mirror and tell yourself your script isn't finished. It's only just started.

Tell yourself rewrites will make it better. YOU will make it better. You will listen to feedback, you will think about it, you will see if multiple sets of feedback point to common issues, and you will leave your ego and all other defense mechanisms in another room. Listening, learning, thinking is important here.

Step two – Get someone else to read your script. Actually, that's a big part of step one, but I felt like it needed its own step.

Anyone really, as long as they know they are reading a draft, and they are expected to provide feedback. So probably not your Mom. Or your cat. Maybe a script competition, maybe someone like me – a script coach, or, if you have no money, a writer friend. Yes, it's handy to have writer friends – so you can read their stuff and they can read yours.

Between your own feedback (after you take a moment and reread), and notes from someone with some sort of clue, you'll start to get a sense of what's working, and what's not working. By the way, when giving notes, it's really useful to point out good bits, not just bad bits. No one likes a list of issues, without some kindness. Give feedback the way you would like to receive feedback. It's my main philosophy, along with giving writers somewhere to go/something to think about. No one wants feedback leaving them feeling stuck and hopeless and devoid of ideas to improve their work.

Step three – Absorb the feedback, and start to think about things you might want to experiment with changing, or adding, or subtracting. I know that sounds like it's part of step two – but taking a moment to really let everything sink in deserves its own step. After I had pages go up in my old writing lab mentioned earlier, I would write everything down, then put the notebook away, go to sleep, wake up, and then in the shower, try to remember what feedback I got. I promise you the stuff that came to mind first in the shower were always the issues that genuinely needed work. They were the notes that resonated with me – on a subconscious level. I rarely went back and reread the notes, because I didn't need too. The feedback that needed to stick, stuck.

Step four - Have a go at changing some stuff. We live in a glorious age – where computers keep track of previous drafts. What you have written will never go away, barring some sort of accident. Which means your next draft can take some creative swings. Because you literally have NOTHING to lose. Nothing. Try some stuff. See if you can get the audience to connect more, to engage with your characters more. To FEEL MORE.

I had a conversation with a writer client who said they were worried that inserting too much emotion would make the script "cheesy." They are not the gushy romantic type, and this was a genuine concern. The problem – the scripts they write tend to be a little cold, more plot focused than emotional journey focused. Really well written but harder to engage with.

I'm going to tell you what I told them. Shut up and get mushy. That's not exactly what I said. This writer has a spouse – so I suggested exploring their relationship. Every couple has their own inside jokes, their own shorthand language, their own rhythm and ways of showing affection and emotion and personal intimacy. And tensions/trigger points. Most don't look like they just left a cheap jewelry TV commercial. I suggested incorporating some of that into the relationship between the couple in the script. Don't be afraid to be authentic, to borrow from your own life.

Nora Ephron did it – and she wrote scripts that weren't cheesy.

My point is the rewrite gives you a moment to try something with zero pressure. The first draft kinda lays down one roadmap – now you get to go off road, dig a little deeper, and try a little harder to explore the human experience.

Just a reminder – I have never given a note where I said "I felt too much." I have never read a script where I thought "stop it, I'm too emotional." So I challenge you to try and get to that point.

Try a new draft where you focus specifically on feelings, where you really dig into the emotional journeys of the characters, and you try writing a scene that makes you genuinely uncomfortable, no matter the genre. Put aside your "cheesy" worries – because you can always dial it back in the next draft.

Here's the fun thing about these kind of rewrites – even if you don't keep what you write, I'm pretty certain it will open new doors for you on multiple levels. You will get to know your characters in new and interesting ways. You will give them opportunities to express themselves in ways you may not fully predict. You will push them to reveal more about who they are, and what your story is doing to them. They will become more authentic, simply by you spending more time with them.

At the same time, check in with your own emotional connection to your story. Is this draft giving you the "feels" you want it too? Sometimes I can get lost down story rabbit holes, and after a while I look at what my script has become, and I have to ask "is this what I wanted to say? Is this scratching the itch that compelled me to spend this much time writing a draft? Am I exploring what I originally wanted to explore, in a way that feels real, and appropriate?" If the answer is "maybe" to any of those questions, your rewrite can address those concerns.

Everyone's approach to rewriting is different. Mine – I tend to do page one rewrites – which means I rebuild the entire script from page one. I find plugging scenes in here or there can sometimes lead to other issues developing. Plot holes, character inconsistencies, etc. So I usually bite the bullet and start all over. But then I tend to write quickly – and I know that. You do what works for you – you'll figure it out the more you do it. Just make sure you do it.

You also want to avoid simply "reacting." If someone like me points out some issues with a character or a situation, resist the urge to just shove in some new words in one scene and call it a new draft. That's not listening, that's reacting, and your script risks becoming a "dog's breakfast" (it's a saying where I come from), which is a cute expression for a mess.

Rewriting is fun. It's challenging, it provides great opportunities, and it develops a skill set you absolutely need. Ultimately, it helps you stay in touch with your audience on an emotional level.

And here's the final secret to help you embrace this process. If you've done all the work we've been talking about in this book, chances are you have a pretty good take on what your story is "about" on an emotional level. You understand what aspect of the human condition you are exploring. Or at least are trying to explore. Which means when you get feedback from someone – a friend, a professional, an industry executive – you can quickly decide if their suggestions and thoughts are helpful, in relation to your underlying theme and emotional journey, or not.

Which is a long way of saying if you get feedback that doesn't mess with your theme or journeys, then don't be too precious about incorporating them. You'll make the exec happy, and you aren't violating the reasons you wrote the script. But, if you are exploring the power of love to bring new hope in life, and the note giver wants the film to be about how love sucks and everyone should live alone and avoid getting hurt, then you can have a more substantive conversation. Which you can have pretty easily, because you know what you're doing and trying to achieve. You can articulate your theme. And if the person doesn't get it, or doesn't want to get it, and wants instead to tell you the script they think you should write – then you have a choice to make. You can either thank your Mom and make her dinner and never talk about your script again, or if it's someone willing to write you a check – you can decide what matters more – your emotional theme, or the chance to get paid. I'm not giving you an answer to that question – because it's too hard, and there are too many variables.

But I will say that producer who wanted my father/son script to become a mother/son script withdrew the option – not because they were angry or we had a fight, more that after lengthy conversations (and I mean lengthy) they came to realize it was actually an entirely different movie they were seeing in their head, and that the dynamics of those relationships are naturally different. It was a fascinating experience, but only possible because I was able to articulate what I was aiming to explore.

One more quick anecdote – another producer wanted to option another of my scripts, but they were eager to fit the story into more of a Young Adult (YA) genre format, and in the draft they read, my two lead characters do a lot of swearing and talk about kinda "adult" stuff at times. When the question about rewriting was asked, my initial, knee-jerk response in my head was "absolutely not." I felt like there was no way I was going to de-fang my script and make it suitable for children. Or whatever Young Adults are these days.

Fortunately, I kept those thoughts in my head and allowed myself to think. What became obvious soon after was making some shifts and changes wouldn't actually mess with any of the themes of the script. Removing swear words and changing the ages of the central characters would make the script easier to sell, without harming my initial intentions. So why on earth would I not make those changes? I still have my expletive-filled draft, yet to be filmed.

Do you see the differences? Turning a father/son story into a mother/son requires a very different relationship, which messes with the script's original intention. Taking out swear words whilst keeping the original themes and making the project more attractive to genre buyers makes total sense.

Sometimes, as writers, we get a bit stubborn or a bit willful or a bit defensive, which leads us to confuse these two situations, or see them as identical. So we refuse to rewrite. We refuse to incorporate notes, and we self-sabotage our writing career when a little more thought may have led to a different choice.

Which all means the more you know what your script is "about," the clearer you are with your purpose for the project, what aspects of the human condition you hope to examine, and what you want to say, the easier it is to figure out the differences between a rewrite that will enhance your career, and a rewrite that will ruin your original idea.

And then...magically...rewriting becomes your friend, not your sworn enemy.

One final tip about knowing when to let go of a draft and declare it "finished" – There's no easy answer. There may not be a true "moment" where you look at it and think "I'm done." Unless there is. For me, it's more about hitting the point where you feel the script is saying what you want it to say and you've had enough feedback to feel a certain confidence that the script is standing on its own two feet, that it's resonating with strangers. There'll always be a feeling that you can add this or subtract that or whatever. But if you feel it's hitting the emotional journey you wanted, then it's okay to let it go, until someone offers you money to re-write it.

Because it's important to keep writing new material. Your emotional landscape is always evolving. So it should always be informing your writing. Feel free to keep coming back to an old script – especially if it attracts attention, but try to keep moving into other projects, other emotional spaces. Every new idea and new draft is an opportunity for growth on so many levels – and rewriting can grind into a dead zone, where you get a little obsessed with tinkering at the edges, rather than diving head first into an entirely new idea.

But as a general rule, if you've done a bunch of pretty comprehensive drafts (a bunch can mean whatever you want it to mean, but let's go with 10), then it's either in pretty solid shape, or it's not coming together the way you want. At which point you either stop tinkering, and show people and feel good, or you shelve it, and circle back around in a few months if you are still feeling the desire. Either way, it's time to put it down, pat yourself on the back, and start thinking about the next idea.

12

HOPE

This is it! The final chapter. The part of the book where we focus on the positives, and leave you feeling inspired and excited to dive into your idea or your next draft!

The underlying aim of this book has always been to give you more tools for your writing toolbox, to help you focus your attention on the really important bits of this whole screenwriting caper, and to more fully appreciate and embrace all the work that's involved, on levels that may not feel obvious at first.

I know so many screenwriting books tell you what you should do, or not do, and many contradict each other. Which can leave you feeling confused, overwhelmed, and even worse...stuck. No one wants to be confused about which way to turn. It leaves you feeling powerless, lacking confidence, and awful. It's an easy hole to fall into, especially with a ragtag group of book writing experts leading you in complicated circles with threats of immediate failure if you don't follow an incomprehensible chart. At least my predictions of doom are easy fixes!

So let's use this moment together, at the end of a book, to focus on all the positive things, to remember why we do this, to acknowledge the challenges and obstacles, and to feel good about putting in the work to overcome them as best we can. I mean, what else are we going to do, plant tomatoes?

The most important thing a screenwriter needs is not a book on writing. Or a template on a three-act structure. Or another book on writing. Or even a laptop and a coffee shop that has cheap parking and lets you sit there for hours without buying much actual coffee. Although the last one is super helpful.

The most important thing a writer needs is...passion. Enough passion to overcome the self doubts, the anxieties and the second guessing we all do. That feeling, deep inside, that this is a project worth sticking with. That this often really frustrating process is something worth believing in, worth persevering with, worth doing. It's the passion for the idea that is the underlying reason we do this.

I say this because when you are faced with too much information, too many choices, too many opinions, too many thoughts, it's okay to step back a moment, and gather some perspective. At the end of the day, writing is about feeding that passion, about finding a way to satisfy that inner voice, that driving rhythm in your brain that makes it really hard not to write. I don't know if you're like me, but often when I'm working on a new idea, I have moments that flash in my head. Feelings mostly. Stuff I hope I can get onto the page – and make others feel what I think I can make them feel, because I'm feeling it. Being able to create that tone, or those scenes, that fully deliver what I think and feel. It's a driving passion of mine, one that is rarely achieved – at least on the first draft.

There are many times during the outline process, and even the first draft, where I'll stop, and wonder if I'm achieving what I originally set out to achieve. I try to step back and see if I've gotten myself too lost in the weeds of structure or subtext or logistics or whatever. To see if I've moved too far away from my original idea, the one that made me passionate enough to want to devote hours and hours of essentially free labor to try and bring to life.

Often the answer is yes, I have moved too far away. Or I've started to shackle myself, or my characters. I've started to play it safe, to conform to what I think people will like, not what I want. At that point I stop. I'll go for a walk, listen to different music, and try to reconnect with what I wanted to say.

One thing I have discovered in all these decades of writing in all formats – I connect with an audience far more completely when I connect with myself. When I am able to challenge, confront, and entertain me, I pretty much always bring strangers along for the ride. When I focus too much attention on trying to give people what they want, it ends up being meek, thin, wishy-washy, or worse..."cute." Don't settle for cute. Never settle for cute.

But as mentioned previously, don't get too lost in the self-pleasuring. The easy fix is to make sure your passion also includes a fierce desire to entertain strangers, and share all the feelings and story elements and everything else with people you don't know.

The thing I love most about being a journalist is that feeling of being able to tell people stuff I've just learned. To be the first to let them know what's going on is as cool a feeling as anything else the job entails. Screenwriting passion really should be no different. To want to share what you feel about something with others is really important and often overlooked or downplayed.

As you feel all the passion for the idea, expand the feeling to include strangers. Embrace and enjoy that desire to share your passion with others. That way everyone wins. You get to enjoy your idea, and really dive into satisfying yourself, while never letting go of those around you. It's the whole "Hey guys, let me tell you this AMAZING story!" We all get caught up in someone's passion for their story and their passion for telling us the story. If it's just someone self indulgently exploring something that singularly pleases them, they effectively shut us out of the story, and things don't go well. Passion for the story and the storytelling!

A quick reminder not to go too far the other way too – there really is a lot of balancing to be done when writing. You want to avoid surrendering your own passions for the perceived will of the people. Your passion comes first, then find ways to include everyone else. If you suppress your passion – you risk pandering to the crowd, and no one wants you to do that – least of all me. We, as an audience buy into someone's creative vision much more readily than someone's idea of what we might want to see that doesn't involve any genuine passion anywhere. Movies by committee rarely succeed as well as the committee hopes.

The next positive take away – once you embrace the process, and de-mystify, or de-romanticize it (I may have just invented a word), the more enjoyable it becomes.

This writing thing is work. It's often not super fun, and success on any level is never guaranteed. But the quicker you let go of the dreamy fantasy of sitting in a coffee shop, or a shed out the back, gnawing softly on a pencil as you type a one draft masterpiece, beloved by all, the quicker you'll develop a healthy and more satisfying process.

No one in the history of writing has ever delivered first draft masterpieces. No one. Even people who wrote before typewriters were invented still scratched stuff out and rewrote. Writing in some ways is closer to stone polishing than whatever fantasies exist out there. Writing is all about committing to exploring your idea. It's a process. Just like life.

We live every day. Some days are awesome. Some days are dog shit. Most days are fairly calm and mundane. We make mistakes, we get things right, we grow, we change, we evolve. Just like your screenplay. Just like your children. Just like your relationships.

So rather than getting frustrated about not reaching the finish line quickly enough, try to embrace the process. Sometimes, often actually, screenplays take time. Your first idea may not be complete enough. You may need to time to marinate on some things until a solution appears. Process. Patience. Just because you gave yourself two hours today to figure out your third act climax problems, and you didn't find something you like, doesn't mean you won't tomorrow.

There's a saying allegedly from Dorothy Parker – "I hate writing, but I love having written." Most writers share that feeling most days, no matter how much you accept the process. I'm not suggesting you're going to tiptoe through tulip fields feeling warm and fuzzy about outlining. Or writing a scene that exposes your deepest, darkest anxieties. What I am suggesting is by understanding all that is involved, you can move writing to more like a job. Work. Something you work at. Not purely a creative endeavor where a muse sits on your shoulder and genius pours onto the page. Because if you believe that, you will write something lazy, you will show it to someone too soon, it will not be well received, you'll get annoyed, defensive and frustrated, and you may feel an urge to give up. Or resist rewrites.

What you are trying to do is get a job. That requires training and experience. Like any job.

Wanna know the best way to train for this job you want? Write stuff. Then write more stuff.

The more you write, the less pressure attached to each word, the less pressure attached to each script. Just write. Practice. Try stuff. Make mistakes. Write some more. These are all just words on a page. None of this defines you as a human being. None. Of. It.

If you write something, you think it's decent, but someone hates it – big deal. They don't hate you. Even if you poured your emotional soul into the script. It's still not you. Your story didn't connect. Happens all the time. When it happens to you, maybe ask for a few details, see if it makes any sense, or if they are just an idiot, and decide what to do next. You are not your writing. They are words on a page, and the more words you put on more pages, the better writer you will become.

Try different things. Experiment. Create a character who speaks entirely differently. Write a scene randomly. Write non-fiction. Just put words onto a computer screen, or a journal, or a napkin. Words out of your brain and into the world makes you a stronger writer. Being a writer means writing, so get to it.

Oh, I should mention "writing" also includes thinking. Or procrastinating. Don't pay any attention to these show ponies who say they bashed out this many pages in a day or whatever. You may find one day you just can't put anything down on paper/screen that's coherent. That's okay. No need to punish yourself for that. I would suggest writing the gibberish anyway, because it's too easy to start to tell yourself you don't feel like going to the gym, you'll go tomorrow, and then it's next week and you've done nothing. So if you're having a crap day, maybe just sit down for 20 minutes, write drivel, and then watch Netflix. Or eat ice cream. Or go to the gym. There's something to be said for rhythm and routine.

Next reminder on your journey to becoming really good at your job – show your script to people. Or better yet, find a group of friends to read it out loud. Everyone secretly wants to be an actor, so it won't be hard to find willing volunteers. Get used to sharing your work with others. Get comfortable hearing your words out loud. It can be very emotionally confronting at first. Terrifying. That's why we practice. First few times you hear someone reading your words you will feel vulnerable and exposed and nervous. I felt like that the first time a newsreader read a script I wrote on TV, even when it was a boring news story about some protest or something.

The more you share your words, the more often you hear them out loud, the more disconnected you get from them. The less power they have over your general self-esteem. The more they become something separate from you, as if they are their own entity, something for the world – and the easier it is to look at them with a more objective eye.

I gotta say, directing a play from my own script was fascinating on that level. I would sit in the theatre with a crowd, watch amazing actors who had rehearsed and rehearsed and rehearsed, and all of a sudden the script was no longer mine. It was theirs. It was the audiences. It didn't belong to me. It was its own thing. Which took away a lot of stress and worry.

Write something, and get friends to read it out loud. They'll probably suck at it – big deal. Bring snacks. Make it a fun afternoon. Listen to their comments afterward. Understand it may veer into "group think" and head in directions you neither expect nor appreciate. Don't get defensive. What do they know? Remember, they are trying to help. Show your words to friends – hopefully people in different social circles, ages, genders. See if you get similar comments (assuming people read it – sadly you're going to need patience on that front).

Enter competitions. Don't spend a fortune – just enter comps that offer prizes you like. Get some written feedback if you can afford it. Not a lot – no need to waste too much money. But this is a great way to learn about how your script is working with strangers who have nothing to do with you. You'll be able to quickly tell if they are reacting on an emotional level. If they are connecting with the characters, going along for the story ride, engaging in the way you want them to engage. This is an important learning tool – as you hone your craft and build your abilities to connect with an audience. Which as I may have mentioned is pretty much the reason we do this.

Don't sit in your bunker and assume everyone is an idiot and no one gets you if the script isn't universally beloved. Remember, this is a process. Embrace the process. It's going to take some time to get good at this. Which is okay.

You'll be able to track your progress. You'll learn to feel the room as your script is being read. You'll figure out which notes are helpful and which are stupid. None of this is instinctual. All of it is learned by doing. So, you know...do.

A great friend of mine who has produced so many movies I can't count anymore, once responded to some whining of mine about my lack of success or progress with one word. She looked at me and said, "Quit." I looked at her a bit confused. She said, "If you're so miserable and frustrated, just quit. People quit every day. No one's going to notice, or miss you."

I remember sitting back on my chair.

"You're doing this because you want too. If you don't want to do it anymore, you don't have too. But if you do decide to continue – understand it's your choice. Your decision.'

And what she didn't say because she's lovely was – so stop whining.

It was great advice for those hard writing days. Knowing this is a choice I'm making, so it's in my best interests to do what I can to get better – is helpful. I offer that to you as we end this book. If you don't like what you're doing, just quit. If you decide not to quit, then do what you can to improve your skills. Think about your audience, embrace your command and control over their emotional experience. Dig deep into your own emotional experience. Find the connection with your story.

That doesn't mean write autobiographies. Connection comes in many forms. Let's say you are intrigued about a story involving a kid from a small town moving to the big city and feeling lost and alone. Maybe you never lived in a small town. But you know what it's like to feel like an outsider. Someone who may not immediately belong wherever you happen to be. Tap into those feelings, as you do research to figure out the larger plot elements. Find the way you are emotionally connected to the story you want to tell.

Not only does that make a more authentic emotional backstory to your script, the simple truth is producers and representatives love that. If you're able to have a meeting and say "Yeah, I really connected with Mary's story because I moved schools when I was fourteen, and it was a really rough year, and I felt isolated and alone" – you will win the meeting. Even if the script is about a sponge on another planet that has talking avocadoes.

If you connect with your story and characters, it's way easier to connect your audience. That authenticity is everything.

———

So to sum up this entire book, always pay attention to the audience, and always pay attention to you. The more of you poured into your pages, the more your script will resonate with the audience. Both elements are crucial to honing your craft as a writer ready to earn a living from your craft. Ignore either of them, and you risk doom.

That's it. That's all I got on this topic. I hope there were some useful bits in here for you. Once you understand the basic structure and what's required, you can start to build solid outlines, then expand into drafts, and see what happens! I have total faith that the more you do this, the better you'll be, and the more committed you are to the process, the more willing you are to learn, grow, make mistakes and keep digging deep, the better the chances you'll be ready when your opportunity comes. From what I've seen, there is an excellent chance an opportunity will come...the challenge is to make the most of it.

Remember, you are a writer. Your task it to entertain strangers, and move them emotionally in ways they don't expect. Because that's what we all want as audience members...including you. We want connection, we want the shared experience, and you have the desire, talent and work ethic to deliver something truly special. What an amazingly fun and profound opportunity.

You've got this. I have no doubt at all.

Thanks for reading. Good luck. Now go write something!

ONE MORE THING

Get Tim to read your script!

As you know by now, Tim is a highly respected script coach, and does his best to provide a pair of fresh eyes and helpful thoughts on any script. If you would like Tim to read your script and deliver written feedback, or feedback with a follow up zoom conversation, or just want to schedule a chat to work through your idea, just email him at tim@write-la.com. He looks forward to helping!

Tim has also developed a range of in person seminars to support the lessons in this book and accepts a limited number of speaking and workshop engagements each year. Content and durations can be customized to meet your needs. To learn how you can bring Tim to your writing group, conference or organization, email tim@write-la.com or visit www.write-la.com.